Angels

In Scripture
and Tradition

Owen F. Cummings

Paulist Press
New York / Mahwah, NJ

Library of Congress Cataloging-in-Publication Data
Names: Cummings, Owen F., author.
Title: Angels : in scripture and tradition / Owen F. Cummings.
Description: New York / Mahwah, NJ : Paulist Press, 2023. | Includes bibliographical references. | Summary: "This book presents a solid Catholic teaching about angels through Scripture and Tradition"—Provided by publisher.
Identifiers: LCCN 2022029924 (print) | LCCN 2022029925 (ebook) | ISBN 9780809156337 (paperback) | ISBN 9780809187959 (ebook)
Subjects: LCSH: Angels—Catholic Church.
Classification: LCC BT966.3 .C86 2023 (print) | LCC BT966.3 (ebook) | DDC 235/.3—dc23/eng/20221104
LC record available at https://lccn.loc.gov/2022029924
LC ebook record available at https://lccn.loc.gov/2022029925

ISBN 978-0-8091-5633-7 (paperback)
ISBN 978-0-8091-8795-9 (e-book)

Published by Paulist Press
997 Macarthur Boulevard
Mahwah, New Jersey 07430
www.paulistpress.com

Printed and bound in the
United States of America

Contents

Preface

> There is this gap between the world, the ancient
> innocent world in which angels might walk with
> man, might appear at any moment, and our kind of
> industrialized world in which they cannot.
>
> Cornelius Ernst, OP[1]

Toward the end of the Creed every Sunday, Catholics profess belief in "one, holy, catholic and apostolic church." That implies believing what the church teaches, and a compendium of the church's teachings may be found in the *Catechism of the Catholic Church*. At the same time, however, Catholics do not approach because they cannot approach the teaching of the church with what we might call "an empty head." In other words, we necessarily approach the teaching of the church within the context of our own culture and experience, with all that that entails.

I doubt if there was ever an age when Catholics did not ask questions about their faith. In the earliest Christian document, St. Paul's First Letter to the Thessalonians in the fifties of the first century, we find Christians asking questions about the Parousia. In the experience of these Christians the expectation of Christ's imminent return in glory was being called into doubt not least because some in their community had died. One of their questions was, "What will happen to our dead who will not be present for this event?" In the letter St. Paul offers his reassurance that those who have died will not be disadvantaged at the time of the Lord's final appearance. One could go on to document questions that Christians in every generation have raised about their received faith, the doctrines of the faith, their moral beliefs, and so forth. The entire Christian tradition would be nothing but indoctrination if all the Christian had to do was receive it in an unreflective, unquestioning manner. Nurture in our faith, in a way that is appropriate for adults and in the context of the shifting shapes of culture, demands a certain interrogative quality.

Theologian Nicholas Lash (1934–2020) has grasped this understanding of theology with great lucidity when he writes of the theologian's task and responsibility as follows, including a little humor.

> Theologians are usually elderly, or at least middle-aged. The theologian's audience, therefore, has a right to expect of him a measure of scholarly expertise: they are entitled to assume that he knows a number of things that other people either do not know or have forgotten. Moreover, the theologian's audience also has a right to expect of him a measure of that wisdom which is the fruit of experience and suffering....It is, I believe, part of the theologian's responsibility, a function of his expertise and his measure of wisdom, to try to ask, and to help other people to ask, fundamental questions as a matter of personal concern....People often complain that too many academic theologians, instead of building up the faith and strengthening the

hope of the ordinary Christian, spend their time, at best, wrapped in cocoons of academic abstraction and technicality and, at worst, "knocking" or undermining the beliefs of the person in the pew.[2]

Observant readers will not only recognize the gentle humor in Lash's position, but also that theologians, at least these days, are certainly not all elderly or middle-aged or male, but I hope that such readers will also be aware that Nicholas Lash loves the church, loves the teaching of the church, and throughout his life agonized to present persuasive accounts of the church's doctrinal tradition for modern people.

If we acknowledge truth in Lash's description of theology and of the theologian's task, as I do, then two consequences seem to me to follow. The first consequence is that the theologian must know as carefully as possible the church's doctrinal tradition. Now, no one and no lifetime is capable of absorbing with due diligence all that the church teaches in every respect. Those who study theology need judiciously and prudently to select those issues, those doctrines, those periods of church history, with which they wish to engage. That means that their conclusions, their positions should end with a comma, rather than with a period. There is always so much more to be understood in any theologian's understanding and this theologian wishes to be emphatic about that in the positions expressed in this book. The second consequence is that the theologian must use God-given intelligence to sift through past understandings of the church's doctrinal tradition in order to arrive at, one hopes, a more persuasive account of the issues for her/his time and audience. If the account given proves to be persuasive and helpful, that is wonderful. If not, then that unpersuasive account should be left to one side and discarded.

ANGELS

These introductory remarks provide the framework for this exploration of the theology of angels. One of my grandchildren asked me some time ago, "Grandad, are angels real?" The child was trying to sort out for herself how fictional characters in children's literature and cartoons and video games were to be distinguished from the invisible reality of angels. I had to think about this quite a bit, and I recalled a comment from a former colleague in religious education, John M. Hull: "The art of theological conversation with young children is under-developed, and this goes for much of the Christian education in churches as well as homes."[3] The intention throughout this little book about angels is to be helpful to contemporary Catholics, especially perhaps catechists for all age groups whose energies help to hand on the faith to others, to develop the art of theological conversation. It is certainly not intended in any way to be destructive of Catholic faith. The desire rather is to invite Catholics to a more mature and more adult appreciation of the rich gift of faith. In reaching toward this more adult understanding, it may well be the case for some people that they will feel pushed out of their doctrinal comfort zones, but I think that is a risk worth taking. My readers must judge for themselves.

1

Angels Today, Really!

In accepting the Bible as authoritative we would do
well to pay serious attention to the whole problem of
angelology....Any intelligent person is likely to be
deterred by the fear of having to wade through the
enormous pile of nonsense which has accumulated
in the field of angelology over the ages. No other
theological subject has been so much the victim of
so much unbridled imagination of generations of
teachers and preachers....

    If the belief in angels is a religious phenomenon
that must needs be taken seriously, the same can be
said of the unbelief in angels. In other words, how is it
possible that both angelologists and anti-angelologists
profess themselves to belong to one and the same
religion?

Rob van der Hart, OP[1]

Tradition maintains that an openness to the angelic
presences can transform our attitudes and activities
toward wholeness, creativity, and a charity which is at
once exacting and joyous.

Aidan Nichols, OP[2]

INTRODUCTION

Growing up, many of us learned by heart the prayer to our guardian angel: "Angel of God, my guardian dear, to whom God's love commits me here. Ever this day be at my side, to light and guard, to rule and guide. Amen." Now grown, one might wonder what this beautiful little prayer still means. I suppose one might choose to disregard or even discard such childhood religious practices. Or, alternatively, one might choose to probe a little further the meaning of such prayer practices. This little volume of "Angel Thoughts" is a choice of the alternative way. In our enormously pluralistic world, with its myriad philosophies and outlooks, it is to say the least interesting to think about angels and how they might feature in the Christian symbol system.

"Angels in one form or another are found in most religions of the world, but most prominently in the religions of the book, such as Zoroastrianism, Judaism, Christianity, and Islam. Whether as messengers, companions, guardians, guides, overseers, or members of the heavenly court, they assist the divine-human encounter, while their malevolent counterparts, demons or fallen angels, endure it."[3] Broadly speaking, then, angels are to be found in the traditions of these major Middle Eastern religious traditions. Apart from Judaism in the Old Testament, however, the concern of this little volume will be with the Christian tradition, and how angels might be understood and interpreted by Catholics today. Of course, as well as the possibility of disregarding or discarding "angel thoughts," one might prefer to hold on to cherished childish religious inheritances, without much critical reflection. For many, however, that is not a realistic option. Many wish to examine, or reexamine, such precious inheritances in the light of ongoing personal experience and growth. That is what these few pages are attempting to do.

Right away it seems important to say that given the "hierarchy of truths" from Vatican II, angels are nowhere near the top of that hierarchy! Nonetheless, they feature in both ordinary conversation and in Christian people's spirituality, and perhaps even in the wider popular culture and so, to say nothing more, they are worthy of a theologian's attention.

Angels make their appearance at the celebration of every Eucharist at the end of the preface—"and so we join with all the angels and saints"—and at the Sanctus, "Holy, holy, holy Lord God of hosts...." They are called upon in a funeral in the anthem, "May the angels lead you into Paradise." His guardian angel leads the recently deceased Gerontius to the throne of God in John Henry Newman's epic poem "The Dream of Gerontius."[4] The Pulitzer Prize–winning play and 2001 movie *Wit* provides us with a particularly moving example of the "presence" of angels. Vivian Bearing (played by Emma Thompson), a professor of English literature who specializes in the poetry of John Donne, has been diagnosed with terminal ovarian cancer. As Vivian lies dying all alone in her hospital bed, she is visited by her former professor, Evelyn Ashford, her mentor. Professor Ashford climbs up onto Vivian's sickbed and reads to her from the children's book *The Runaway Bunny*. As the visit ends, Professor Ashford bends down to kiss Vivian and she says to her, "Time to go. Flights of angels sing thee to thy rest." The words are taken from William Shakespeare, *Hamlet*, Act V, in which Horatio speaks to Hamlet in death: "Goodnight sweet prince. Flights of angels sing thee to thy rest." Ashford and Horatio, of course, are but echoing the *In Paradisum* of the Christian funeral. Very beautiful sentiments about angels, but are they real? Are angels real? If they are, who or what are they? What purpose if any do they serve, especially with regard to humankind?

OPENING UP BELIEF IN ANGELS

Let us turn to the remarks of theologians Rob van der Hart and Aidan Nichols at the head of this chapter. What they have to say are good ways to open up Christian belief in angels. Van der Hart is making three important points. First, that angels appear throughout the Scriptures and so merit careful attention. Second, that "an enormous pile of nonsense has accumulated in the field of angelology over the ages," something that is fairly easily verified. Third, that the position of those who profess unbelief in angels equally needs to be taken seriously. Nichols focuses on the benefits that accrue from an openness to angels. These points will be given close attention in the following pages.

In our Christian tradition angels are found throughout the Scriptures. As already noted, angels are mentioned at the heart of the Mass, in the Sanctus, and in our funeral liturgies we commit our loved ones into the care of the angels, "May the angels lead you into paradise…." One author, Carol Zaleski, points out that "The liturgy is the richest source for a Catholic theology of angels; yet current liturgical writing is strangely neglectful of the role of angels in worship."[5] I think Zaleski is right about liturgy as "the richest source for a Catholic theology of angels," but the absence of angels is not only a characteristic of "current liturgical writing" but arguably of theology in general.

The absence of angels in theology does not find a parallel in popular sentiment and culture. One thinks, for example, not only of *Wit*, but also of the television series *Touched by an Angel*, or other movies such as *City of Angels*. Then there are the novels featuring angels by the late Fr. Andrew Greeley (1928–2013). If one goes to the Amazon website to find out about angels, there is a legion of entries in terms of books, novels, and movies of various kinds. The very existence of these materials sparks the question for me, "Is this the *sensus fidelium / the sense of the faithful* at work?" Could it be that the imaginative (and other) interest of ordinary people is somehow keeping alive, albeit not always in healthy ways, traditional concerns and beliefs about angels, even as the theological academy shows little interest? Perhaps. It may even be the case that this popular belief in angels might pave the way to a deeper encounter with God, something to which Dominican theologian Dominic White draws attention in the following statement:

> Nevertheless, in cases which admit of no rational grounds for dismissing someone's report of having seen an angel, I suggest that, with appropriate discernment, we should treat this as God's invitation to complete the work of evangelizing that person which he has already begun through the heavenly church. If we begin by ridiculing reports of angelic apparitions, we cannot be surprised if their subjects are alienated from the church and take refuge in the vagaries of the New Age. But if we respond eirenically, biblically, and rationally, they are more likely to be drawn to the Bread of Life.[6]

Those are very good adverbs—"eirenically, biblically and rationally." My hope is that along with the views of van der Hart, Nichols, and White this little book will treat of angels "eirenically, biblically and rationally," drawing upon the work of specialist scholars.

Since at least the time of St. Anselm of Canterbury (1033/34–1109) theology has been defined as "faith seeking understanding." It is very important to pay careful attention to this definition. The definition views theology as seeking "understanding," not "explanation." Explanation is a further reach beyond understanding. Explanation we might say intends a complete and comprehensive conceptual grasp of something, whereas understanding is more open-ended, reaching out toward mystery, if you like, an ever-present excess of understanding. As one theologian has it, "this is at once an astonishingly bold assertion, and a soberingly modest one. It is bold in its insistence that, by God's gift, we are enabled to have some understanding of the unfathomable mystery (of God and the things of God.)"[7] Thus, "some understanding," not "explanation." This is the understanding of theology within which this little book on angels is set.

This way of understanding theology seems to me to demand a double requirement of the theologian: first, and this is a lifetime's work, to assimilate as comprehensively as possible the multilayered tradition that is Catholicism; and second, to sift with critical care through this assimilation, reaching toward a "faithfully traditional understanding." Both poles of the enterprise are equally necessary, the openness to receive what we have been given by the tradition of those who have gone before us, *and* the critical evaluation of what has been received. In the pages that follow I hope to have honored both poles.

2

Angels in Scripture

The Old Testament

Scripture assumes familiarity with beings variously called "angels," that is to say, "messengers," "men," "Yahweh's host," "heavenly host," according to their function, their appearance, or their relation to God. In the post-exilic period they are more precisely conceived as "sons of God," "gods," "princes," "powers," "spirits," which either have no body or only one that is apparent. They come as God's messengers to aid or punish, are assigned to the individual person or nation, and often have a name of their own (Michael, Gabriel, Raphael, Uriel).

Karl Rahner-Herbert Vorgrimler[1]

It is false to assume that the Old Testament writers, however exalted their conception of the Godhead might be, conceived of God as alone in isolated majesty over against men, the creatures of his will. There is ample evidence to show that this conception of monotheism was held in conjunction with a belief in a spiritual world peopled with supernatural and superhuman beings who, in some ways, shared the nature, though not the being of God.

D. S. Russell[2]

INTRODUCTION

Let us start by acknowledging right away that the world of the Bible is not our world. "We belong to the twentieth century. We don't belong to the biblical world. It is a great mistake to suppose that we do. We belong to quite a different sort of world. And if we want in some way to enter into the biblical world we have got to go through a fairly complicated kind of process."[3] This is not the place to enter into the complicated kind of process that is the science of biblical interpretation. That would take us much too far from our concern with angels. Nonetheless, our two opening quotations provide us with a very helpful way to explore the meaning of angels in the Old Testament Scriptures. From the Rahner-Vorgrimler dictionary we get a very precise and full description of the terms used for angels in the Old Testament as well as their functions. The second opening quotation from the late scholar of Jewish intertestamental literature, D. S. Russell, helps us to realize that Jewish monotheism is not synonymous with God being entirely on his own, as it were. The latter part of the quotation is particularly interesting. Although the words "supernatural and superhuman" can be interpreted in various ways, in this context they may be said to refer to what today might be called "spiritual beings," although that term itself requires further parsing. Even more interesting is Russell's claim that these "spiritual beings" shared the nature of God. That statement opens up a very interesting world of theological exploration, but first things first.

The English word *angel* comes from the Latin word *angelus* which is a transcription of the Greek word *angelos*, and this Greek word is used in the Septuagint, the Greek translation of the Hebrew Old Testament, for the Hebrew word *mal'ak*. It is usually translated as "messenger." It is this meaning of "messenger of God" that seems to be the earliest form of Old Testament belief in angels. It is often suggested that belief in angels was not originally part of the Hebrew theological tradition but rather something that entered into that tradition as a result of the Babylonian exile in the sixth century BC. The suggestion continues that God in Hebrew theology had become so transcendent, so otherworldly, that some kind of intermediaries were necessary to make contact with the world of humankind and, hence, the angels. There is some truth in this but it seems to be the case that angels/"spiritual beings" formed part of the Hebrew tradition from earliest times and did not simply enter into that tradition as a result of the religious and cultural contacts and influences of the exile and later.[4]

PASSAGES REFERRING TO "ANGELS"

The following is a list of the major places in the Old Testament where we read about these messengers of God.[5] The messenger

- Appears to Hagar in the desert (Gen 16:7ff.; 21:17ff.).
- Prevents Abraham from sacrificing his son Isaac (Gen 22:11ff.).

- Protects Abraham's slave on his journey to find a wife for Isaac (Gen 24:7, 40).
- Speaks to Jacob in a dream (Gen 31:11).
- Protects Jacob from all harm (Gen 48:16).
- Wrestles with Jacob at Penuel (Gen 32:24ff.).
- Appears to Moses at the burning bush (Exod 3:2).
- Leads Israel through the Red Sea and the desert (Exod 14:19; 23:20; 33:2; Num 20:16).
- Halts Balaam on his way to Balak (Num 22:22ff.).
- Appears to Joshua near Jericho (Josh 5:13ff.) as "commander of the army of the Lord."
- Speaks to the Israelites at Bochim (Judg 5:23).
- Calls upon the Israelites to curse Meroz (Judg 5:23).
- Appears to Gideon (Judg 6:11ff.).
- Appears to the mother of Samson (Judg 13:3ff.).
- Appears to David at the threshing floor of Araunah (2 Sam 24:16ff.; 1 Chr 21:15ff.).
- Appears to a prophet of Bethel (1 Kgs 13:18).
- Appears to Elijah on his way to Horeb (1 Kgs 19:7).
- Appears to Elijah before his meeting with the messengers of Ahaziah (2 Kgs1:15).
- Slays the Assyrians before Jerusalem (2 Kgs 19:35; 2 Chr 32:21; Isa 37:36).

What one needs to do is to read through these references and passages with care so as to begin to grasp just how widespread they are, both across the biblical books themselves and also across the various time periods that they represent in the history of Israel. Having taken that as done, one might move on to the comment of the biblical scholar John McKenzie who has this to say:

> From these passages it is clear that the messenger of Yahweh (in some passages *Elohim*, God) belongs to the earliest part of Hebrew tradition. That the messenger occurs less and less frequently as the story advances is explained by the fact that the earlier traditions are folklore which often heighten the wonderful and appeal to the divine to explain phenomena. It is also clear that the messenger of Yahweh is not clearly distinguished from Yahweh himself (in various passages)....In some of the passages it may be suspected that the messenger of Yahweh is a theological addition to the narrative, intended to preserve the divine transcendence from too intimate a contact with creatures; other forms of the tradition do not show this scruple. We may conclude that the idea of the messenger in early belief wavers between a hypostatization of the divine attributes or operations and a distinct personal heavenly being.[6]

This very careful summary comment tells us that references to the messenger(s) of God are sometimes a folkloric enhancement of the narrative, and sometimes references to God himself at work, and almost always are somewhat lacking in clear specificity. What is eminently clear, however, is that the messenger—either as an independent entity/emissary or as God himself at work in human affairs—is intended to convey in the strongest possible terms God's saving interest in the Hebrew people and their history.

GENESIS 18:1–5

Genesis 18:1–5 provides an intriguing example. In this ancient text three figures visit Abraham, but who are they? Let's look at the text first of all: "(1) The Lord appeared to Abraham by the oaks of Mamre, as he sat at the entrance of his tent in the heat of the day. (2) He looked up and saw three men standing near him. When he saw them, he ran from the tent entrance to meet them, and bowed down to the ground. (3) He said, 'My lord, if I find favor with you, do not pass by your servant. (4) Let a little water be brought, and wash your feet, and rest yourselves under the tree. (5) Let me bring a little bread, that you may refresh yourselves, and after that you may pass on—since you have come to your servant.' So they said, 'Do as you have said.'"

The passage is intriguing not least in terms of grammar. We are told in verse one that the Lord appeared to Abraham, and yet in verse two when Abraham looks up he sees three men, a plural. Continuing to verse three the three become "My lord," a singular. Later Christian authors will make much of this passage interpreting it in Trinitarian terms, as also did artists and perhaps most famously the Russian iconographer Andrei Rublev (ca. 1360–1430) in his great icon *The Hospitality of Abraham*. Nowhere in this text are the three described as angels but rather as three men, although all subsequent tradition will interpret them as angels, as David Albert Jones notes: "There is clearly something that sets them apart, as Abraham recognizes that 'the Lord' is visiting him, but they are still described as 'men'. These angels have no wings or halos, and they are not named. At this stage in Hebrew thought, as evident in the books of Genesis, Numbers, Judges, and Joshua, angels do not show a great deal of personality. They deliver the message that is given them to deliver, and do what they are sent to do, but they do not have names of their own or stories of their own to distinguish them from other angels."[7]

SOME OTHER PASSAGES

In a number of passages God understood as monarch is accompanied by a heavenly court, just like earthly monarchs were. Think, for example, of this passage from 1 Kings 22:19: "Then Micaiah said, 'Therefore hear the word of the LORD: I saw the LORD sitting on his throne, with all the host of heaven standing beside him to the right and to the left of him." This "host of heaven" is probably to be understood as God's heavenly court and courtiers, and it is easy to see how they could morph into being messengers/"angels" of God. God's courtiers, as it were, are sent by God to deliver his messages or to do his bidding.

Let's look at another passage, the text of 1 Kings 8:10–11: "(10) And when the priests came out of the holy place, a cloud filled the house of the Lord, (11) so that the priests could not stand to minister because of the cloud; for the glory of the Lord filled the house of the LORD." The occasion is when the ark of the Lord, the most intense symbol of God's presence, was brought into the temple in Jerusalem built by Solomon. The text tells us that the cloud, "the glory of the Lord," filled the temple as God took possession of it and made it the premier symbol of his constant presence with his people. Would it, in the light of this passage, be too much of a stretch to think of the term "the angel of the Lord" as referring to some manifestation of God's saving presence? This would seem to be the case if we look back and consider the list of passages noted above. They are really describing in their own ways God's protective custody of his people, and so his constant and saving presence in their midst. In point of fact, it is only when we come to the much later books of the Bible, books like Daniel and Tobit, that we find mention of angels with quite distinctive and particular characteristics.[8]

JESUS THE ANGEL

As Christians read the Old Testament, they discern the conviction that God will send a savior, often called the Messiah. We know now through biblical research that there are different ways of thinking about the Messiah.[9] Perhaps the best-known passage in this respect comes from Isaiah 9:6, a passage that features prominently in the liturgy at Christmas:

> For to us a child is born,
> To us a son is given;
> and the government will be upon his shoulder,
> and his name will be called,
> "Wonderful Counselor, Mighty God,
> Everlasting Father, Prince of Peace."

When the Jewish translators of the Old Testament into Greek, the translation known as the Septuagint, came to this passage, they were challenged about calling the promised savior "mighty God." That would have unacceptably compromised Jewish monotheism. So they changed this messianic title from "mighty God" to "angel of great counsel." As Christianity began to make its way out from Judaism with its Scriptures in Hebrew, Christians relied greatly on the Greek translation, the Septuagint. That meant, as they applied these Isaianic titles to Jesus, that Jesus was the "angel of great counsel," who brought the good news of salvation, inaugurating the kingdom of God. One finds this title for Christ in the second century author Justin Martyr (ca. 100–165), for example.[10] As Christology develops in the Christian tradition, this title becomes obsolete as Christ is understood to be both divine and human and not, therefore, an angel.

RAPHAEL, GABRIEL, MICHAEL

The names of three angels are known in both Testaments: Raphael, Gabriel, and Michael.

Raphael, which means "God heals," occurs in the Book of Tobit. He is the guardian of a journey (Tob 5—6), the healer (Tob 6; 11:1–15), and the one who expels demons (Tob 6:15–17; 8:1–3). He is also one of the seven angels who offer the prayers of God's people and enters the presence of God himself (Tob 12:15). Raphael further occurs in some detail in the apocryphal *Book of Enoch*. There we find two conceptions of archangels. The first conception is of four angels with the names Michael, Gabriel, Raphael, and Uriel or Phanuel (*Enoch* 9:1; 40:9; 70:1ff.), and the second is of seven archangels (*Enoch* 20:3). John McKenzie points out that "in Enoch, Raphael is a hypostatization of the healing power of God, and there is no reason to think that he is anything else in Tobit."[11]

Gabriel means "hero of God" or "El is strong." Gabriel is never called an archangel in the Scriptures, although he is one of the named archangels in the apocryphal *Book of Enoch*. In the Book of Daniel 8:16–26, Gabriel is the angel who interprets the vision of the ram and the he-goat, and in Daniel 9:21–27 he interprets the meaning of the seventy years of captivity. Gabriel also appears in the New Testament. He appears in the infancy narrative in the Gospel of St. Luke as the angel who announces the birth of John the Baptist to Zechariah (Luke 1:11–20) and the virginal conception of Jesus to Mary (Luke 1:26–38).

Michael means "Who is like God" or "Who is like El." In Daniel 10:13 we read as Michael assists Gabriel, "But the prince of the kingdom of Persia opposed me twenty-one days. So Michael, one of the chief princes, came to help me, and I left him there with the prince of the kingdom of Persia." Then just a few verses farther along in Daniel 10:21: "There is no one with me who contends against these princes except Michael, your Prince," and in Daniel 12:1: "At that time Michael, the great prince, the protector of your people, shall arise." Michael in these passages is thought of as the heavenly spirit or agent who watches over and protects the Jewish people.[12] In the New Testament, in the Book of Revelation 12:7, Michael is the leader of the angels in the battle between the dragon and his angels.

Putting these ideas and insights together we conclude that what we are dealing with in these postexilic texts are ways of naming various aspects of God in relation to humans. Thus, Michael/Micha-el represents God's overcoming evil; Gabriel/ Gabri-el stands for God's communicating with us; Raphael/ Rapha-el is God watching over and guiding us. Our childhood prayer immediately comes to mind: "Angel of God, my guardian dear, to whom God's love commits me here. Ever this day be at my side, to light and guard, to rule and guide."

Theologian Bernard Cooke writes, "Such divine activity we may believe, is very real; but that need not mean that there are 'real persons' who bear such names....Still the tendency to personify persisted. Some of the aspects of Yahweh's action on behalf of his people came to be personified, possibly as Michael or Gabriel or Raphael."[13]

DEVELOPMENTS WITH THE BOOK OF DANIEL AND OTHERS

The Book of Daniel, although its setting is during the period of the Babylonian exile, was written much later in the time of the revolt of the Maccabees, around 165 BC. "The book of Daniel marks an important stage in the development of ideas about angels. It has a concept of different ranks of angels and of angels appointed to watch over different cities and nations."[14] The Book of Tobit, probably written about 200 BC, was essentially a moral tale and one in which the angel Raphael is a key actor. The *Book of Enoch*, different parts of which were written between 300 and 100 BC, was a centrally important and very popular text in Jewish apocalyptic literature. It is in this book that we find the names of seven archangels: Uriel, Raphael, Raguel, Michael, Saraquel, Gabriel, and Remiel. This book also tells us the story of the fall of the angels and it is quoted in the New Testament in the Letter of Jude, a very short text of some twenty-five verses. In verses 14–15 we read, "(14) It was also about these that Enoch, in the seventh generation from Adam, prophesied saying, 'See, the Lord is coming with ten thousands of his holy ones, (15) to execute judgment on all, and to convict everyone of all the deeds of ungodliness that they have committed in such an ungodly way, and of all the harsh things that ungodly sinners have spoken against him.'"

During the time after the Babylonian exile when the books of Daniel, Tobit, and *Enoch* were being written, Jewish scribes in the Egyptian city of Alexandria were engaged in translating the Hebrew Scriptures into Greek, the translation that became known as the Septuagint. "The Septuagint translation was used at the time when the Jews were becoming more interested in angels, and so it tends to add in references to angels that are not explicit in the original."[15] One of the clearest examples of this tendency may be found in Deuteronomy 32:8. The NRSV translation of this verse reads as follows: "When the Most High apportioned the nations, when he divided humankind, he fixed the boundaries of the peoples according to the number of the gods." However, the Septuagint translation reads a little differently: "When the Most High established the bounds of the nations according to the number of the angels of God." It is easy to see the difference—the Hebrew text makes no mention of the angels of God, but the Septuagint does. Times have changed, and now Jewish thinkers are more interested in angels. This leads theologian David Albert Jones to say: "The period after the return from exile saw a shift in Jewish views on angels: there was a greater concern with hierarchies, ranks, or numbers of angels; there was a growing devotion to a particular guardian angel assigned to each person; there was increasing talk about demons and the figure of a chief of demons, the Satan, the enemy of God and of humankind; finally, there was a fascination with the names of angels."[16]

WHAT ABOUT SATAN?

"Both the Hebrew word Satan and its Greek equivalent *Diabolos* (devil) means something like 'accuser' or 'slanderer' or 'adversary'. The name belongs to that official who brings man before the court and tries to demonstrate in front of the judge and the jurors man's wickedness."[17] In other words, Satan is, at least in earlier stages of the Hebrew theological tradition, just an official in God's heavenly court, and in that capacity is neither good nor bad. Think, for example, of the text of Zechariah 3:1ff.: "Then he showed me the high priest Joshua standing before the angel of the Lord, and Satan standing at his right hand to accuse him." Satan here is the prosecuting attorney, as it were, in God's court. We find the same idea in Job 2:1: "One day the heavenly beings came to present themselves before the Lord, and Satan also came among them to present himself before the LORD." And so, at least in part to such texts as these we are mistaken when we look upon Satan simply as the great opponent of Yahweh.

As biblical traditions develop over time, we find a number of unpleasant mythological figures will become associated with a view of Satan as evil. Among these are the following:

- Belial. In 2 Corinthians 6:14, it is a name which means originally "the worthless one." Beliar is the name of the demon often found in apocalyptic literature. Etymologically the name is probably compounded of two words meaning "it is of no profit."[18]

- Beelzebul, or in some manuscripts Beelzebub. It occurs in Matthew 12:24 and is in origin a Syrian god. The comment by John McKenzie is particularly instructive. This is what he writes, "The meaning of the Hebrew name is most easily explained as 'lord of flies,' which is scarcely the original title of the (Syrian) god; it is more probably a Hebrew contemptuous corruption of the divine name. This name is almost certainly correctly preserved in the New Testament. Beelzebul was formerly explained from the Hebrew word *zebul*, 'habitation.' It is now explained from the Ugaritic *zbl*, 'prince,' a title frequently given to Aleyan Baal, the fertility god of Ugarit."[19]
- Lucifer, as in Luke 10:18. He was originally the king of Babylon and above all the serpent who stands for all that is supposed to the well-being of humans. He is also the great dragon and deceiver of the world in Revelation 12:9.

While we shall comment a little further on the nature of the devil, this book does not focus on the later developments of demonology. That would require a volume in its own right, and there are good and solid publications on this.[20] From the reflections in this chapter we may say that angels in earlier biblical times seem to be representations of God's loving care and presence, and in later postexilic times, they begin to develop individual identities and names.

3

Apocalyptic Literature
and Angels

I think it might not be wholly without use to look
at the extra-biblical parallels to what we take to be
angels in the Bible.

Cornelius Ernst[1]

When we enter the inter-testamental period we
find that belief in angels has grown to proportions
unknown in the Old Testament writings. Details of
their numbers, their names, their functions, their
natures are given which, though in many cases
having their beginnings in the canonical Scriptures,
far outstrip anything to be found there. Among
the apocryphal books by far the greatest interest in
angelology is taken by the apocalyptic writings.

D. S. Russell[2]

THE WORD *APOCALYPTIC*

The word *apocalyptic* has been used already in this book. What exactly does it mean? *Apocalyptic* comes from the Greek verb *apokalypto*, which means "to reveal, to disclose," thus giving us the Greek noun *apokalypsis*, meaning "revelation, disclosure." "Apocalyptic" is a form of literature widely found in Judaism between about 200 BC to AD 200, which purports to reveal or disclose the future. The literature is usually pseudonymous, that is to say, it is usually proposed under the name of a past celebrity such as Enoch or Moses. Moses, of course, is familiar to all Christians but Enoch may not be. Enoch had a certain fascination in ancient Judaism, much of it stemming from his description in the Book of Genesis 5:21–24: "(21) When Enoch had lived sixty-five years, he became the father of Methuselah. (22) Enoch walked with God after the birth of Methuselah three hundred years, and had other sons and daughters. (23) Thus all the days of Enoch were three hundred and sixty-five years. (24) Enoch walked with God; then he was no more, because God took him." Enoch now becomes a mysterious figure, taken by God, and for reasons obvious from this rather cryptic text gives rise to all kinds of speculative literature, most especially the *Book of Enoch*.

Fr. Henry Wansbrough, the English Benedictine New Testament scholar, provides us with a good description of apocalyptic literature. "Apocalyptic writing is characteristic of oppressed societies which find themselves in humanly hopeless situations, promising them deliverance and salvation by some sort of supernatural transformation. In the biblical sphere it occurs principally at three moments, the Babylonian Exile (586–548 BC), the persecution by the Syrian king Antiochus

Epiphanes (167–160 BC), and the time leading up to the two Jewish revolts of 66 and 132 A.D."[3] The primary purpose of apocalyptic literature is to generate hope, most especially for oppressed people who feel entirely hopeless. The language of apocalyptic is both symbolic and secret, and is to be understood only by the elect, those chosen by God. In terms of Holy Scripture the revelations of apocalyptic are not meant to be factual description of the future. Recognizing the literary genre "apocalyptic" means that we do not approach such literature to find specific details concerning the future—hope, yes and always; a blueprint of the future, no. Rather, apocalyptic writings are intended to provide for God's chosen ones encouragement and hope in the midst of their present or future sufferings when everything looks bleak and hopeless. When the language and the symbols and the images of apocalyptic literature are taken literally, they can give rise to all kinds of bizarre speculations, and can become in their own fashion quite dangerous. As we recognize the stylistic elements and characteristics of apocalyptic, we should pay attention to an important caution from the Old Testament scholar John Collins. He makes the following point about biblical language in general when he says, "Biblical scholarship in general has suffered from a preoccupation with the referential aspects of language and with the factual information that can be extracted from a text. Such an attitude is especially detrimental to the study of poetic and mythological material, which is expressive language, articulating feelings and attitudes rather than describing reality in an objective way." Collins goes on to point out that "the apocalyptic literature provides a rather clear example of language that is expressive rather than referential, symbolic rather than factual."[4] Collins is telling us that we are too preoccupied with factual information provided by biblical language in general, and, by way of contrast, more careful attention to poetic and mythological language would serve us better. Notice another emphasis that Collins is making here—apocalyptic literature does not provide us with a detailed understanding of an unknown future, but rather helps to articulate and to confirm a basic conviction that no matter how difficult the present time is, the future is in God's hands, and that future, therefore, is secure. Angels are prominent in this literary genre of apocalyptic as agents of God's protection and deliverance.

ANGELS IN APOCALYPTIC LITERATURE

D. S. Russell was one of the most important students of apocalyptic literature in the mid-twentieth century.[5] Having studied intensively all the major apocalyptic books, Russell sets out to provide a systematic analysis of their contents. In this analysis he has a detailed chapter entitled "Angels and Demons," and to this I am much indebted, though my concern here is more with the angels, not the demons. Russell writes, "In the inter-testamental period, particularly as illustrated by the apocalyptic writings, there is a remarkable development in Jewish thought concerning the world of spirits and angelic beings generally." Various reasons for this development come into play. First of all, the growing transcendence of God in postexilic literature led to a need for some kind of bridge between the transcendent God and his creation. Second, the problem of evil and suffering also played a role, and this was due in large measure to the influence of Persian religious mythology (Zoroastrianism). The idea already existed in

Hebrew thought that God had given authority over the nations of the world to the angels. Now there developed the notion that some of his angels had taken the power into their own hands with the following result described by Russell in these words: "No longer were they (the angels) simply God's envoys to whom he gave the charge of punishing those who denied his rule; they themselves became part of the rebellious family and took upon themselves the right to reign. They refused any longer to take their orders from God, but were either rulers in their own right or were prepared to take their orders from someone other than God who, like themselves, had rebelled against the Almighty." And so Russell concludes, "Thus the problem of human suffering was seen to be but part of the greater problem of cosmic evil. Every part of the created universe was affected by it, and human life had to be lived out under its shadow.... Human life and the life of the universe were in the grip of malignant powers who had wrested the authority from the hands of God."[6] Within this context, Satan as the prosecuting attorney in God's heavenly court now becomes the evil archenemy of God. This developing and varied angelology, according to Russell, is impossible to systematize, but we can pick out various elements of it to illustrate how the tradition is developing.

One of the first things we can note is that the angels are arranged in a kind of hierarchy that is similar to an earthly army with its officers and various ranks. In the noncanonical *Book of Jubilees*, often dated between 165–150 BC, we read the following:

> [God] created...the angels of the presence and the
> angels of sanctification, and the angels of the spirit
> of fire and the angels of the spirit of the winds, and
> the angels of the spirit of the clouds, and of darkness,

25

and of snow and of hail and of hoar frost, and the angels of the voices and of the thunder and of the lightning, and the angels of the spirits of cold and of heat, and of winter and of spring and of autumn and of summer, and of all the spirits of his creatures which are in the heavens and on the earth.[7]

The first thing we notice in this passage is that the angels are all God's creatures, they are not in some sense independent entities. Again, we see that these angels mediate God's power and authority over every aspect of creation, and so in that sense serve to protect both God's transcendence and immanence, God's presence throughout creation. Yet again, we can notice a certain hierarchical ordering of the angels. First are "the angels of the presence"; second come "The angels of sanctification," and these are followed by a third ranking, the angels who are set over the natural world.

In this hierarchical ordering of angels, angels were believed to represent the various nations of the world in heaven. We find this idea in the Book of Daniel where we read in chapter 10,

(12) [The heavenly messenger] said to me, "Do not fear, Daniel, for from the first day that you set your mind to gain understanding and to humble yourself before your God, your words have been heard, and I have come because of your words. (13) But the prince of the kingdom of Persia opposed me twenty-one days. So Michael, one of the chief princes, came to help me and I left him there with the prince of the kingdom of Persia, (14) and I have come to help you understand what is to happen to your people at the

end of days. For there is a further vision for those days."...(21) But I am to tell you what is inscribed in the book of truth. There is no one with me who contends against these princes except Michael, your prince.

Following on through Daniel 12:1 we find that Michael is further described: "At that time Michael, the great prince, the protector of your people, shall arise." The nations of the world have their guardian angels—"princes" as they are called in this text—and Michael was thought to have had a special responsibility as the guardian angel of Israel. This is what is being communicated to Daniel by the heavenly messenger.

MOVING INTO THE NEW TESTAMENT, BRIEFLY

These developing Jewish ideas about angels were inherited by the earliest Christians. In some New Testament texts we find the saving work of Christ being interpreted as his triumph over the angelic powers. We seem to find this idea present in the Letter to the Ephesians, 1:20–21: "(20) God put this power to work in Christ when he raised him from the dead and seated him at his right hand in the heavenly places, (21) far above all rule and authority and power and dominion, and above every name that is named, not only in this age but also in the age to come." The nouns found in verse 21, *rule, authority, power,* and *dominion,* are references to various ranks of angels. The same notion is found in Colossians 2:15: "(Christ) disarmed the rulers and authorities and made a public example of them, triumphing over them...." It is never doubted in these texts that Christ is supreme over these angelic powers. What is interesting for our purpose is the very existence of these angelic powers, a legacy from the earliest strata of Jewish Christianity. The existence of these angelic powers is simply taken for granted, and the apocalyptic developments of angelology should be understood in particular as taken for granted by the earliest Christians. The malevolent dimension of angelology/the demonic world is also taken for granted, but Christ is absolutely supreme over all of these angelic powers, both positive and negative.

4

Angels in Scripture

The New Testament

Even after the Christian church had separated from the rest of the Jewish community, the beliefs and practices of early Christianity were very much in continuity with Judaism. This is seen in relation to angels. Christian beliefs about angels are typical for Jews of their day.

David Albert Jones[1]

THE PASSAGES CONCERNING ANGELS

What we find in the Testament about angels generally follows the lines of Old Testament and apocalyptic literature. The following summary provides all the relevant passages, and it would be good to read through all of them.

- *Angels serve as messengers*: Matthew 1:20; 2:13, 19; Luke 1:11ff., 26ff.; 2:9ff.; Galatians 3:19; Hebrews 1:4ff.; 2:2.
- *Angels serve as guardians and protectors*: Matthew 4:11; 18:10; Mark 1:13; Luke 22:43; Acts 5:19; 12:7.
- *Angels serve the divine court*: Matthew 24:36; Luke 12:8ff.; 15:10.
- *Angels serve as companions of Christ as judge*: Matthew 13:41–49; 16:27; 24:31; Mark 8:38; 13:27; Luke 9:26; 2 Thessalonians 1:7; 1 Timothy 5:21.
- *Angels bear witness to events of salvation and particularly to Jesus's resurrection*: Matthew 28:2; Luke 24:23; John 20:12; Acts 8:26; 10:3ff.; 27:23; 1 Corinthians 4:9.
- *Angels are agents of healing and of destruction*: John 5:4; Acts 12:23.
- *Angels offer worship to God*: 1 Corinthians 11:10.

Many contemporary scholars would find the origin of the Gospels as we now have them within the eucharistic assemblies of the early church. It is within these house-churches gathered for Eucharist that memories of Jesus would have been shared, catechesis conducted albeit in a rudimentary state in the first century, and the entire fund of Jesus's teachings passed on from one generation to the next. In a very real sense, the Gospels were formed in the setting of the Eucharist, as the earliest Christian communities shared their memories of and reflections concerning our Lord Jesus Christ.

ANGELS IN THE NEW TESTAMENT

The conception of the angels in the Gospels does not advance beyond the Old Testament conception, and in some ways is less imaginative. The angel is still primarily a messenger or a member of the heavenly retinue, and there is not always a sharp distinction between the angel as a personal being and as a personification of the divine word or the divine action….In the New Testament as in the Old Testament the angel is sometimes no more than another word for a divine communication or a divine operation personified.[2]

These are the words of the scripture scholar, John McKenzie, and they offer a very succinct summary of angels in the New Testament. There is no great distinction in the Gospel narratives concerning angels between angels as actual realities in their own right and angels as personifications of God's presence in word or in action. The primary meaning of angels is always the closeness of God's loving presence to humankind.

This is what we find in the infancy narratives in the Gospels of Matthew and Luke. Angels warn St. Joseph of the coming birth of the child Jesus (Matt 1:20) and then later of the flight into Egypt (Matt 2:13), and then finally of the return to Nazareth. In this respect the angel is not significantly different from the "messenger of the Lord" found in the Old Testament, and the angel in the Matthew narrative is unnamed. In the Gospel of St. Luke the angel of the infancy narrative is named. His name is Gabriel. He announces the birth of John the Baptist to Zechariah (Luke 1:11–20), and then he announces the conception, birth, and the mission of Jesus to Mary (Luke 1:26–38). John McKenzie comments, "Gabriel is probably chosen here because it is the only angelic name of the Old Testament which is connected with the messianic fulfillment. Gabriel appears several times in the books of Enoch, but not as a messenger.

His appearance in Luke is modeled after his mission in Daniel and is conceived as the completion of his mission in Daniel."[3] Reading the text of Luke further, we find the "angel of the Lord" appearing to the shepherds and announcing the birth of Jesus to them, "a Savior, who is the Messiah" (Luke 2:11). Luke 2:13–14 continues: "Suddenly there was with the angel a multitude of the heavenly host, praising God and saying, 'Glory to God in the highest heaven, and on earth peace among those whom he favors!'" "Here again," maintains McKenzie, "we are in Old Testament conceptions."[4]

Leaving the infancy narratives behind and moving further into the Gospel text we find a number of references to angels. Let us take as given, as most New Testament scholars do, that Matthew and Luke relied upon Mark's Gospel as they composed their own. When we approach the pericope of the temptation of Jesus we find the angels, but not in all of the gospel traditions. Mark tells us that "the Spirit immediately drove [Jesus] out into the wilderness. He was in the wilderness forty days, tempted by Satan; and he was with the wild beasts; and the angels ministered to him" (Mark 1:12–13). Matthew expands this very brief narrative of Mark's and then ends with the following words, "Then the devil left him, and suddenly angels came and waited on him" (Matt 4:11). Like Matthew, the evangelist Luke expands on the temptation narrative in Mark, but unlike Mark and Matthew, Luke does not mention angels ministering to Jesus after the temptation. Instead, Luke's pericope ends as follows: "When the devil had finished every test, he departed from [Jesus] until an opportune time" (Luke 4:13). Although the line is missing in several important manuscripts of St. Luke's Gospel, the New Revised Standard Version, in the context of Jesus's agony in the garden of Gethsemane, reads, "Then an angel from heaven appeared to him

[Jesus] and gave him strength" (Luke 22:43). Angels appear again at the resurrection of Jesus, but they were seen by only a few—Matthew 28:2; Luke 24:23; John 20:12. In these verses angels are quite definitely "messengers."

When we come to the last book of the Bible, the Book of Revelation, we find angels aplenty. Scripture scholar, Fr. Wilfrid Harrington, OP, the veteran Irish biblical scholar, writes of angels in this book, "In short, in Revelation angels are omnipresent. Predominantly, they operate as messengers; it is their traditional role, indicated by the very name *angelos*. If at times they are clothed in majesty, that is but a reflection of the word or deed they speak or do at the divine bidding. They are, patently, symbols of God's variegated communication with his creation and, more particularly, with his world of humankind."[5] Twice in this book, when John the Seer falls down prostrate before an angel, the angel corrects him: "No, not that! I am a fellow servant with you and your comrades" (Rev 19:10; 22:8–9). Revelation 4:8–11 has the angels celebrating what we might call a perpetual liturgy:

> And the four living creatures, each of them with six wings, are full of eyes all around and inside. Day and night without ceasing they sing, "Holy, holy, holy, the Lord God the Almighty, who was and is and is to come." And whenever the living creatures give glory and honor and thanks to the one who is seated on the throne, who lives forever and ever, the twenty-four elders fall before the one who is seated on the throne and worship the one who lives forever and ever; they cast their crowns before the throne, singing,

You are worthy, our Lord and God,
   to receive glory and honor and power,
for you created all things,
   and by your will they existed and were created."

THE CHALLENGE POSED BY THE TEXTS

With the aid of biblical commentaries, we can explore in greater depth the meanings of these individual passages and references to angels, and that kind of exploration is of great value. At the same time, given everything that has been said already about angels in the Old Testament and in the inter-testamental apocalyptic literature, some immediate questions present themselves: What are we moderns to make of these texts today? With all the advances that have been made in the interpretation of the Scriptures, how are we to decide what is referential, that is to say, objectively given, from what is to be understood as more symbolic, acknowledging, of course, that the symbolic is real, very real indeed, and not to be misunderstood as purely imaginative? Such questions seem to me simply unavoidable, even if the responses cannot be simply black-and-white, in mathematically clear terms. In all of this, I believe, we are handicapped by centuries (at least, if not millennia) of misconstruing the "real" with "what is out there now," as if our imaginations (not to be thought of as a fantasy world) did not disclose reality.

Although he is speaking about angels in the infancy narratives of St. Matthew and St. Luke and in the resurrection narratives, systematic theologian Bernard Cooke offers some helpful comments in this regard. This is what he says: "Very briefly, both the infancy narratives describing Jesus' birth and the accounts of Jesus' resurrection are special forms of literature that cannot be treated as if they were simply factual descriptions of something that happened. Something did happen, something of unparalleled importance, but something beyond the power of ordinary language to convey; so, story and metaphor are used. This means, however, that we cannot argue from the text to establish the actuality of details in the account."[6]

The position reached by the author is this: Angels function in most of the ways described especially in the Old and New Testament texts as symbolic mediations of God's loving care for humankind. As far as the biblical texts themselves are concerned, these symbolic mediations/angels are undoubtedly real because God's loving care is the absolute foundation of all reality. Not all Christians will accept this position, but it is a position that in the terms of the Scriptures I cannot avoid. In a subsequent chapter I will provide some argumentation that will offer the possibility of reaching *beyond* this horizon of the symbolic, but without excluding it.

5

Angels in the Christian Tradition

Thomas Aquinas produced the most well-developed
and sustained account, indeed the single most
influential account, there has ever been of the nature
of an angel.

David Albert Jones[1]

INTRODUCTION

St. Thomas Aquinas may have indeed produced the most well-developed and sustained account of angels, as David Jones suggests, but he was heir to a long Christian tradition of thinking. The creation of the angels is usually located in Christian theology with the beginning of creation generally. Think of the words of Genesis 1:1: "In the beginning…God created the heavens and the earth." In Christian tradition "the heavens" came to be understood as "all things invisible," as the Creed has it. They were generally thought to be spiritual creatures with intellect and will, creatures without bodies.

When we move out of the New Testament period (assuming, of course, the Old Testament Scriptures), subsequent Christian authors take the reality of angels for granted. This immensely rich Christian period did not make the post-Enlightenment differentiations with which we are familiar between what is "objectively real" and what is "symbolic interpretation." That world did not yet exist. The symbolic was real and the real was symbolic; it was a both-and theological world rather than an either-or one. One theological author puts it helpfully as follows:

> Beneath the surface of distorting neo-Platonic suppositions, patristic-medieval speculation also preserved the original biblical view [of angels]. Indeed, the tasks the Fathers assigned the angels are transparently those belonging either to the Trinity in its direct gracious presence to human persons or to Christians themselves in their ministry to one another. These tasks range from inner enlightenment of the soul to ministries of the ecclesial community, such as guiding catechumens through the process of initiation. On the whole, then, the angels of the Bible are not so much intermediaries as accompaniments to the divine-human partnership, a position that emerges in polemical response to other views assigning a more decisive role to the angels.[2]

One clause in that last sentence is particularly interesting— "the angels of the Bible are not so much intermediaries as accompaniments to the divine-human partnership." Accompaniments to the divine-human partnership? That seems to me not particularly different from affirming that angels are symbolic representations of God's immense love and care for his human creatures.

We find the following description of angels in the Rahner-Vorgrimler dictionary with regard to the Christian tradition:

> The Fathers defend the created nature of the angels against Greek and Jewish apocalyptic notions: they do not as in various forms of Gnosis take part in the creation of the world, but are nevertheless more powerful than men. The purely spiritual nature of the angels becomes a thesis of angelology (St. Thomas Aquinas) on the occasion of a definition of the Fourth Lateran Council which presupposes the existence of the angels.[3]

This is a very helpful launching pad for our selective exploration of angels in the Christian tradition. Rahner and Vorgrimler insist on three points:

1. That the fathers of the early Christian tradition are pretty well unanimous in affirming that angels are creatures, and do not enjoy any kind of autonomous existence apart from God their Creator.
2. Angels are more powerful than human beings and their nature is purely spiritual, something affirmed by St. Thomas Aquinas in particular.
3. The existence of angels is presupposed by the Fourth Lateran Council in 1215.

THE PATRISTIC PERIOD

With regard to Rahner and Vorgrimler's first point, the most complete and yet accessible theological synthesis of angels in the patristic tradition remains that of Jean Daniélou, SJ's *The Angels and Their Mission*.[4] In the introduction to his book, Daniélou shows himself aware of two contemporary pitfalls in the understanding of angels. He writes, "The first comes from the rationalists who group angels and demons together as personifications of psychological realities and who would like to see in them a mythical interpretation of data to which psychoanalysis would furnish the key. Others, justifiably reacting against these tendencies, show a lively interest in the invisible world; but they seek to penetrate by means of spiritism or theosophy, and, by their imprudent attempts, they stray from the one single way of access that is given to us: Jesus Christ."[5] Perhaps, adapting Daniélou somewhat, we might say that his position is opposed to on the one hand rationalism/skepticism and, on the other, an uncritical approach to the meaning of angels. As a well-established patristic scholar, Daniélou contrasts the patristic approach with that of later theologians. "It has often seemed to us as we read the Fathers of the church, that the circumstances of their times drew their attention to several questions that later theologians have felt no need to examine at any great length. In angelology, their attention was focused less upon the nature of the angels and their function as adoring spirits than upon their missions to humanity at different moments in the history of salvation."[6] Further, while acknowledging that the Christian doctrine of the angels is a continuation of the traditions of the Old Testament and Second Temple Judaism, he goes on to point out the "fittingness" of angels in the early centuries of Christianity: "The existence of ministers intermediate between God and man fitted itself with advantage into the spreading philosophical systems of Neo-Platonism, the occult religious systems of the Orient that had long plagued the Empire, and even the Roman mind itself with its pantheon of greater and lesser deities."[7]

In ten excellent and succinct chapters, Daniélou synthesizes what these early Christian theologians have to say: The Angels and the Law; The Angels and the World Religion; The Angels of the Nativity; The Angels of the Ascension; The Angels and the Church; The Angels and the Sacraments; The Guardian Angel; The Angels and the Spiritual Life; The Angels and Death; The Angels and the Second Coming. This is a very fine resumé of what the fathers of the church have to say about angels, and the interested reader is referred to Daniélou's book for details. He provides very ample quotations from the fathers, but perhaps lacks a certain critical evaluation. His book is, to say the least, both informative in terms of patristic reflection and very edifying. This is especially the case with the chapter entitled "The Angels and Death."

Daniélou points out that in the Christian tradition biblical ideas conjoined with pagan Greek ideas helped to develop an understanding of angels as accompanying the soul after death into the heavenly life beyond. In the New Testament, for example, we think of Lazarus being carried by angels to the bosom of Abraham (Luke16:22) and "the Greeks were familiar with *psychopompoi*, or soul-escorting angels, who accompany the soul, after its death, toward its heavenly abode."[8] St. John Chrysostom is cited as claiming that just as we need a guide in this life when traveling from one city to another, so the soul needs a guide as it passes from this life to the next. Similarly, St. Gregory of Nyssa tells of his dying sister Macrina praying for the angel of light to assist her passage to the place of eternal rest.[9] We find echoes of this comforting idea in the anthem at the end of the Mass for the Dead, *In Paradisum*, "May the angels lead you into Paradise." It is particularly moving when sung in the traditional Latin version. It is also most beautifully rendered in St. John Henry Newman's epic poem *The Dream of Gerontius*. An elderly Christian, Gerontius, is on the point of death and he is afraid. After death his guardian angel guides him to the House of Judgment where he realizes that God is nothing but Love.[10] What a wonderful tradition from Lazarus to Newman, and what a comfort to Christians moving toward death. In my judgment the persistence of this tradition of the angels accompanying the dead into final and full communion with God is a fine witness to its truth. Now we move on to give attention, albeit briefly, to the following authors who speak of angels: St. Augustine, Pseudo-Dionysius, and St. Thomas Aquinas.

ST. AUGUSTINE (354–430)

For Augustine of Hippo, probably the most influential theologian of Western Christianity, angels formed an essential portion of his vision of creation....Between God who is immutable and the bodily world of mutability in both space and time, there was for Augustine, as a logical part of a complete creation, a world of beings who because they were not bodily were not spatially mutable, but though pure spirits were still mutable in time (or its equivalent). These, of course, were the angels. As Augustine's theology passed on to shape the Christian belief and theology of the

Middle Ages and beyond, so, too, did his explanation of the angels.[11]

A recent monograph by theologian Elizabeth Klein, *Augustine's Theology of Angels*, provides an extremely detailed account of what the saint has to say about the angels, and I am much in her debt here.[12] What Jean Daniélou did for the patristic theology of angels in general, Elizabeth Klein has done for St. Augustine in detail. She says, "Any reader of Augustine will know that his thought is so complex and his theological ideas are woven together in such an intricate way that when one attempts to pull out a common thread of any given topic, one is in danger in undertaking the task of unraveling the whole."[13]

Augustine thinks of the angels as created light, based on the phrase in the creation account of the Book of Genesis, "let there be light." Since all creation comes to be through the Eternal Word, the Word that became incarnate in the Lord Jesus, as created light, then, the angels receive their light from the creative Word. In a fundamental sense, the very being of the angels for Augustine is oriented toward the incarnation of the Word. The angels read the Word of God forever.

"They consult God when they act, as we do in prayer. And their habit of praising God in the morning for his creation and recognizing their creaturely status in the evening also corresponds to our praying of the Psalms."[14] In this sense, we may say that our human praying of the Liturgy of the Hours participates in that heavenly/celestial praise of the angels. It is an outpouring of praise and gratitude to the God whose best name is Love and who desires his creation to be in loving communion with himself. This leads Elizabeth Klein to conclude that "given the principle that the angels are created in community and that their life is worship, we should not be surprised to find that worship is also a central issue (if not *the* central issue) of *City of God*."[15] In the City of God, praise and gratitude rule as creatures, angelic and human, adore this loving God. In the earthly city, by way of contrast, human beings are turned in upon themselves, love only themselves, and love others only in relation to themselves. Worship we may say is the absolute foundation of human happiness and flourishing—just as with the angels—with the consequent realization that all of creation is God's gracious and loving gift. Nicely phrased by Elizabeth Klein, the life of the angels is worship, "but in this worship they do not forfeit themselves, rather they gain themselves and are themselves."[16] This holds true for humankind.

"The angelic-human communion which is the church is constantly being sustained by God and constantly offering itself to God in return. On earth, the church learns to make this sacrifice of the heart in the Eucharist, and Augustine describes even the heavenly life of angels with the language of eating. What Christ has become in the incarnation is the milk which provides the sustenance of the altar, but is the very same food which sustains the angels in heaven."[17] What a marvelous vision! The Eucharist makes the church and, while the church made by the Eucharist has a temporal beginning in the entire event of our Lord Jesus Christ, there is, as it were, an eternal Eucharist feasting on the eternal Word for the angels, and this is our human destiny too. As Augustine has it, the Eucharist of our earthly pilgrimage will become the bread of one eternal day.[18]

PSEUDO-DIONYSIUS

"Around the year 500 CE, possibly in Syria, lived a monastic writer whose influence on the Latin West was to be more powerful than any other Eastern mystic."[19] This is the figure known as Pseudo-Dionysius. Who was he? We don't know. His name is taken from Dionysius the Areopagite in Acts 17:34: "But some [of the Athenians] joined [Paul] and became believers, including Dionysius the Areopagite and a woman named Damaris, and others with them." Our sixth-century author took the name of Dionysius, that kind of thing being quite common in Christian antiquity. Whoever he was, he disappears behind Dionysius the disciple of St. Paul and does not include anything about himself into the texts which he authored. "His joy in the radiance of God's glory, his contemplative unfolding of how the church manifests this light, and his profound analysis of how best to speak of this radiance all made him an irresistible figure to generations of theologians."[20] So, if we do not know anything about him personally, we do know, however, that his influence was enormous throughout the medieval period, and his thinking about angels was particularly developed. Although angels are frequently mentioned in patristic literature, there is little speculation about them until Dionysius the Areopagite.

It was his examination of the Scriptures that led him to posit a nine-level angelic hierarchy: angels, archangels, principalities, powers, virtues, dominations, thrones, cherubim, and seraphim. For this writer, this celestial hierarchy was the model for the ecclesiastical hierarchy, the hierarchical ordering of the church. Indeed, the principle of hierarchy was to be found throughout creation. The entire created world was ordered hierarchically, flowing from the sacred hierarchy that is the Trinity.[21] The triune God is the absolute center of all reality and the foundation of all reality for Dionysius. The contemporary scholar of Dionysian theology, Andrew Louth, puts it finely: "Hierarchy is the outreach of God's love, it is not a ladder we struggle up by our own efforts....To depend on God and his love means to depend on other people. It is the members of the hierarchy who purify, illumine, and perfect, and themselves stand in need of such purification, illumination and perfection. The hierarchy is a community that is being saved and mediates salvation."[22] This understanding of hierarchy, then, is a necessary foundation for understanding what Dionysius has to say about angels.

In the angelic arrangement of Dionysius, in descending hierarchical order there were:

- Three choirs of first rank—Seraphim, Cherubim, Thrones.
- Of second rank—dominions, powers, and authorities.
- Of third rank—principalities, archangels, angels.

"The first hierarchy is unconcerned with worldly matters and is completely absorbed in the love of God."[23] The highest rank in this first angelic hierarchy is the Seraphim. The name comes from a Hebrew word, *sarap*, and it means "fire." The Seraphim are the fiery ones, referring to the fire of the love of God. Traditionally, they are associated with the Cherubim, as in the great vision of the prophet Isaiah:

I saw the Lord sitting on a throne, high and lofty; and the hem of his robe filled the temple. Seraphs were in attendance above him; each had six wings: with two they covered their faces, and with two they covered their feet, and with two they flew. And one called to another and said:

"Holy, holy, holy is the Lord of hosts; the whole earth is full of his glory." (Isa 6:1–3)

The second rank is taken up with the government of the world—dominions, powers, and authorities—as their very names suggest. "The third and lowest order of angels is the one most concerned with particular earthly matters. It is here we find the guardian angels and the angels that appear to people."[24] It is possible to see behind Dionysius's angelic ranking the coming together of the divine transcendence and immanence. The highest rank focuses on God's absolute transcendence and, we may say, on God's unknowableness and ineffability, while the second and third ranks give expression to God's immanence, God's gracious and saving presence and outreach to humankind. For Dionysius, the ranks of angels speak of actual angelic entities. However, if we leave aside for a moment the actual existence of angels, his three ranks are really all about God.

The threefold order, reflecting the doctrine of the Trinity, is immediately obvious here. Angels have to do with God's loving and saving outreach. In Dionysius's own words: "The goal of a hierarchy is to enable beings to be as like as possible to God and to be at one with him. A hierarchy has God as its leader of all understanding and action. It is forever looking directly at the comeliness of God. Hierarchy causes its members to be images of God in all respects, to be clear and spotless mirrors reflecting the glow of primordial light and indeed of God himself. It ensures that when its members have received this full and divine splendor they can then pass on this light generously and in accordance with God's will to beings further down the scale."[25] If we moderns, perhaps because of our almost innate egalitarian understanding, are somewhat perplexed by this elaborate, numerical, and hierarchical ordering of the angels, it helps to recognize with this passage that it is all about God offering salvation, that is to say, communion with himself. It is all about God seeking to unite his hierarchically ordered creation with himself. The aim of all hierarchy, and, therefore, the angelic hierarchy, is to bring all beings "into likeness with God or deiformity."[26] The language of Dionysius's various ranks of angels is culled from the Scriptures and other patristic authors and may have little persuasive appeal to modern people. Nonetheless, the very fact that his hierarchical understanding of God and of all creation being persuaded into union with God is thoroughly relational and relates well with contemporary thinking. Contemporary philosophies of the human person, and, indeed, contemporary approaches to cosmology and ecology are thoroughly imbued with the stamp of relationality. All creation, flowing from the relational triune God, is interwoven together, constituting, as it were, an almost infinite web of relationality. In this horizon of understanding Dionysius's nine ranks of angels are best understood as God's gracious creative outpouring of himself inviting the entirety of his creation, albeit in different graded ways, into communion with himself. I believe that this is what the systematic theologian John Macquarrie is getting at when he comments as follows on Dionysius's angelic ordering: "We may reject these thoughts of Dionysius as baseless speculation, but he was correct in viewing the universe in a hierarchical way. This is not a popular conception in our egalitarian age, but it is almost certainly correct in claiming that the beings which exist fall into a graded order. There are rational beings, sentient beings, vegetative beings, a whole range of inanimate beings down to the lowliest subatomic particle. The human race has its place in this series, but it also has its own inner drive to transcendence, understood by the mystic as the quest for God."[27] The angels are there to assist humankind to grow into fuller communion with God.

ST. THOMAS AQUINAS (1225–1274)

In his *The Growth of Medieval Theology*, the third volume of his magisterial five-volume history of the development of Christian doctrine, theologian Jaroslav Pelikan makes the following comment: "Two areas of doctrine that are conventionally associated with the thirteenth century are angels and the church. Even without the help of 'the hoary canard about medieval disputation being chiefly concerned with the number of angelic occupants of the point of a pin,' for which there is no documentation in the texts, the impression is widespread that during this period angelology established itself as a central topic of official church teaching."[28]

"From St. Thomas too, we have speculation on the nature of angels: they are not composed of matter and form; all the angels are each a species; from their immateriality follows their immortality; they can act on a place without movement by applying their power to the place where they want be."[29] The interest in angels in the medieval period stemmed partly from their being pure spirits—with all the attendant metaphysical challenges and issues—and partly also from popular piety in which they played out various roles between God and the cosmos and humankind.

Without doubt, the extremely well-researched volume of the Thomist thinker, Serge-Thomas Bonino, OP, *Angels and Demons, A Catholic Introduction*, provides not only a good, general overview of thinking about angels, but also in particular the angelic theology of St. Thomas Aquinas.[30] For the sake of transparency, however, I have to admit that I find St. Thomas's theology of angels too remote from the way I think. This experienced remoteness has to do with two factors: the (somewhat severe) analytic methodology of Aquinas, and allied to that, the abstract metaphysical approach.

For Aquinas, angels are immaterial, they don't have bodies. The fathers of the church and the earlier medieval theologians considered that angels had some kind of bodies, basing this observation on the biblical narratives concerning angels. Angels were seen and heard in the Bible, and so they must have had bodies of some sort. Not so, says St. Thomas. Distancing himself from earlier thinkers he considers angels to be "pure forms," that is to say they are not composed of matter *and* form, as are other creatures. They are more like God than other creatures, but they are not divine. They are creatures.[31] It might be objected that angels certainly appear to have bodies in the narratives of the Scriptures. Aquinas's reflection on this possible objection may be summarized as follows: "Since an angel is not a body (like a stone or a tree) and has no body either that is united to him by nature (like man), the remaining possibility is that an angel sometimes *assumes* a body. Not because he needs it in order to be what he is, but out of condescension, so as to carry out a mission among men."[32] One might go on to ask, then, how this assumed embodiment comes about. "According to the Common Doctor, an angel forms for himself an *ad hoc* body by condensing the air, which then assumes shape and color, as clouds do."[33] This is certainly interesting, but necessarily very speculative.

When were angels created? St. Thomas's point of view is that God simultaneously created both the visible universe and the invisible universe. "Indeed, according to (Aquinas), the spiritual creation and the visible creation form one universe in which angels and material creatures maintain multiple ties....Something would have been lacking in the angelic world without the physical world and in the physical world without the angelic world."[34] There is an important consequence to this way of thinking for St. Thomas—"angels and men belong to one and the same spiritual society, one and the same church; they commune in one charity while waiting to commune in one and the same beatitude."[35] Both angels and human beings form one spiritual society, one church, in Aquinas's own words: "Where there is one body we must allow that there is one head. Now a multitude ordained to one end, with distinct acts and duties, may be metaphorically called one body. But it is manifest that both men and angels are ordained to one end, which is the glory of the Divine fruition. Hence the mystical body of the church consists not only of men but of angels."[36] This way of thinking provides a much more expansive view of the church, an expansive view that finds expression daily in the Eucharist, for example, in the praying of the Sanctus, and then also in the liturgical calendar on September 29, "Saints Michael, Gabriel and Raphael, Archangels," and on October 2, "The Holy Guardian Angels." These celebrations demonstrate the wonderfully generous creativity of God and his constant loving care for us. These liturgical celebrations, therefore, are important.

FOURTH LATERAN COUNCIL IV, 1215

This is how church historian Brenda Bolton describes the Fourth Lateran Council, called by Pope Innocent III in 1215: "Rome, on the Feast of St. Martin, 11 November 1215, was the setting for a truly great show. There were lights, decorations, music including elephant-sounding trumpets and all types of early thirteenth century razzmatazz but behind it all was a most solemn purpose. All aspects of the show had a liturgical basis. It marked the beginning of the Fourth Lateran Council which was to result in the most important single body of disciplinary and reform legislation ever applied to the Medieval Church."[37] As Bolton points out, this council was the greatest reforming church council of the Middle Ages.

It was also the council that spoke of angels. Here is the pertinent text: "We firmly believe and simply confess that there is only one true God...who by his own omnipotent power from the beginning of time created in the same way both orders of creation, spiritual and corporeal, that is the angelic order and the earthly."[38] No one at the time of Lateran IV really doubted the existence of angels. They were an important presence in both theology and in people's lives and religious experience. This being the case, we might wonder why the council spoke of angels in this fashion. The answer is not hard to find. This conciliar statement was to defend church teaching against the Albigensians, a neo-Gnostic, dualistic, and heretical movement at the time. The council's statement was quite deliberately aimed against the Albigenses, who believed that the angelic world existed from all eternity. The council on the contrary maintained that angels were creatures, and it is the created nature of angels that the council was upholding. This is well expressed by theologian Rob van der Hart who comments helpfully,

> Now, surely, it is a little odd to maintain that the primary purpose of the fathers of this council was solidly to affirm the existence of angels, bearing in mind the fact that among the people they were talking to there was nobody who had any doubt that

angels existed. In fact, the problem was that at that time there were certain people—the Albigenses— who had far too much faith in angels and devils, so much, indeed, that they even denied that they were created by God. The Albigenses maintained that the angelic world existed from all eternity. To counteract this, the council was asserting that angels were creatures.[39]

The church at that time wanted to make clear the belief that the world and everything in it was created by God and that, when it was created, it was "very good" (Gen 1:31). This was a rejection of the dualistic and Manichean/Albigensian idea that there were two gods/principles: a good god/principle and an equally powerful bad god/principle who were involved in constant struggle. This way of understanding the conciliar text about angels defends their createdness and is less concerned to define the existence of angels as such, something no one really questioned. This leads theologian Bernard Cooke, about whom we shall say more in a later chapter, to conclude, "So, as far as I can see and have been able to discover by study, the existence of angels, including guardian angels, is not a matter of required faith; one can be a good believing Christian whether believing in angels or not."[40] In a similar way, Bob Hurd agrees when he says,

> Read out of context, such statements (as in Lateran IV) appear to make the existence of angels binding official teaching, and some theologians continue to interpret them in this way. Read in context, however, it becomes clear that the real point of such statements is to assert that all beings other than God are

created and that evil has a finite, creaturely origin rather than an origin in God. Thus there is room for legitimate differences of opinion about what these teachings intend to clarify and what they require of the believer.[41]

I am inclined to agree with Cooke and Hurd that angels are not binding church teaching in the same way as is the case with the doctrines of the Trinity or the divinity of Christ. At the same time, I believe that they are both missing an important theological insight that has to do with the sheer, creative generosity of God, but a little more about this later.

With the sixteenth-century Reformation there developed quickly suspicion concerning the cult of angels. The Reformation tradition, generally speaking, trimmed away from Christian life everything that seemed who detract from the unique and sole mediation of Jesus Christ. this included the angels, and there was a decline in awareness of and devotion to angels.[42] Perhaps the time has come to revisit the question of angels in a nonpolemical context, eschewing some of the post-Reformation and, indeed, post-Enlightenment suspicions.

6

Angels and the Liturgy

Scripture suggests an engagement between (human
beings and the angels)....We discover Scripture
suggesting that angels and men mix it up with each
other.

David Fagerberg[1]

Here we have...a clear and fundamental locus for
the presence of the angels not simply as it were in
literature but actually in action, because if we believe
in angels at all, this is where we are going to be able to
see them.

Cornelius Ernst, OP[2]

The liturgical theologian David Fagerberg tells us that,
although quite different kinds of creatures, "angels and men
mix it up with each other." He scrolls through the Scriptures—
much as has been done in earlier chapters—to verify and provide details of this "mixing up." He then proceeds to reflect
upon how angels and human beings "liturgize God coopera-
tively."[3] With his impressive grasp of liturgical detail he offers
us much food for thought.

The words of Fr. Cornelius Ernst, an English Dominican and one of the first English-language translators of Karl Rahner, SJ, provide us with a fine segue into a consideration of angels and the liturgy. His essay from which the above quotation is taken is entitled "How to See an Angel." "If we believe in angels at all, this is where we are going to be able to see them." Ernst clearly does not mean seeing angels with our eyes in the ordinary sense, but rather what we might call "seeing with the heart." "Seeing with the heart" is seeing in depth, seeing through the lens of Christian *in-sight*, or, in David Fagerberg's words, "we see (angels) when we look up liturgically."[4]

Angels are in action in the liturgy. One of the earliest representatives of this point of view is the patristic theologian, Origen of Alexandria, who remarks that "There is a double Church present, one of men, the other of angels."[5] The church is more than the people in the pews on a given Sunday, but incipiently all of creation and eschatologically all who are gathered into final communion with God, the angels and the saints, the saints who have gone ahead of us. All are thus present at the liturgy.

THE SANCTUS

Perhaps the most obvious place in the liturgy where we acknowledge the presence of the angels is in the Sanctus, at the beginning of the Eucharistic Prayer. We pray, "Holy, Holy, Holy Lord God of hosts. Heaven and earth are full of your glory. Hosanna in the highest. Blessed is he who comes in the name of the Lord. Hosanna in the highest." In origin this anthem is to be found on the lips of the Seraphim in Isaiah 6:3, where we read of the call of the prophet Isaiah and is continued in the Book of Revelation 4—5.

While the Sanctus has been part of the liturgy since about the fourth century, we do not know exactly when or where it was incorporated into the Liturgy of the Eucharist. Its very liturgical longevity, however, signals its importance, but we may also say that through the Sanctus "there is something cosmic about our Eucharist. It unites heaven and earth."[6] The Sanctus is cosmic in the sense that both in word and thought it brings together the church on earth with the angels in heaven, and also it brings *all of creation* into the praise of God. Let us explore this further.

THEOLOGIANS ON THE SANCTUS

The cosmic dimension of the Sanctus is worth dwelling upon and to help us do so let us call upon the insights and comments of four theologians: Rudolf Otto, Bryan Spinks, Frances M. Young, and Jürgen Moltmann. Rudolf Otto (1869–1937) is well known for his groundbreaking book, *The Idea of the Holy*, in which he wrote in traditional terms of holiness and of the holiness of God in particular.[7] While fully appreciative of the rational side of religion, Otto wished to emphasize the inconceivable, suprarational nature of religion and so of God, and he refers to this as the "numinous." He finds this numinous sense evoked with particular power in the Sanctus. This is what he says: "I have heard the *Sanctus, Sanctus, Sanctus* of the cardinals in St. Peter's, the *Swiat, Swiat, Swiat* in the Kreml Cathedral, and the *Hagios, Hagios, Hagios* of the patriarch in Jerusalem.

In whatever language they resound, these most sublime words that have come from human lips always grip one in the depth of the soul, with a mighty shudder, exciting and calling into play the mystery of the otherworldly latent therein."[8] Otto is referring to the Sanctus as sung in liturgy, both Western and Eastern. The singing of Isaiah's seraphic chorus in the Christian Eucharist was for Otto one of the highest points of awareness of the numinous, of God.

Bryan D. Spinks is an Anglican liturgical theologian teaching at Yale Divinity School. His expertise lies mainly, but not exclusively, in the history of liturgy, Catholic and Reformed, and he has written an outstanding book on the Sanctus from a theological and historical perspective. Here are some of his words about the meaning of the angelic Sanctus: "In giving thanks for the universe, galaxies, planets and life, man, the stuff of the universe made conscious, is rendering thanks to God for his own creation in the *imago dei*, and for all creation."[9] "Hosts" in the Sanctus are understood as the angelic hosts, and this beautiful hymn conjoins the human person, made in the image of God, with those angelic beings in giving thanks to God for who God is, the excessively generous loving Creator of all that is.

Closely allied to the cosmic-liturgical thinking of Bryan Spinks are a few comments of the Methodist patristic scholar and theologian, Frances M. Young. In an essay on the Eucharistic Prayer, she speaks of the Sanctus. "[The Sanctus] comes from Isaiah 6 and the Book of Revelation, and it points to the communion of saints, nay more to the whole creation, angelic and earthly. We are taken up into something which is beyond ourselves. This is not about me, it's not about my church, my fellowship. It is about the whole of God's creation in eternity, and it potentially blows apart all exclusive claims."[10] In this passage, Young, through a reflective praying of the Sanctus, invites Christians to move beyond all their inherited tribalism. With the angels we are taken up "beyond ourselves," into the panoramic expanse of the complete sweep of God's creation.

Finally, we come to the Protestant theologian Jürgen Moltmann. Well known across confessional boundaries for his work in Christology and in Trinitarian theology, Moltmann has similarly fine things to say, at least implicitly, about the angelic Sanctus as a cosmic doxology.

> As God's gifts, all his creatures are fundamentally eucharistic beings also; but the human being is able—and designated—to express the praise of all created things before God. In his own praise he acts as representative for the whole of creation. His thanksgiving, as it were, looses the dumb tongue of nature. It is here that the priestly dimensions of his designations is to be found. So when in the "creation" psalms thanks are offered *for* the sun and the light, *for* the heavens and the fertility of the earth, the human being is thanking God, not merely on his own behalf, but also in the name of heaven and earth and all created beings in them. Through human beings the sun and the moon also glorify the Creator. Through human beings plants and animals adore the Creator too. That is why in the praise of creation the human being sings the cosmic liturgy, and through him the cosmos sings before its Creator the eternal song of creation.[11]

In this passage about creation, all created entities are understood to be eucharistic, that is to say, giving thanks to our

Creator God. Human persons, and we may say angelic beings too—although Moltmann does not mention them explicitly here—have voices, and with those voices render thanks to God for letting them be. All creation is inherently understood to be eucharistic, giving thanks, but humans and angels, conjoined in the Sanctus, have the gift and privilege of hymning this gratitude.

THE *IN PARADISUM*

At the end of the Requiem Mass, as the casket is being carried out of the church for burial, we pray this beautiful prayer for the deceased: In Latin, *In paradisum deducant te Angeli; in tuo adventu suscipiant te martyres, et perducant te in civitatem sanctam Jerusalem. Chorus angelorum te suscipiat, et cum Lazaro quondam paupere æternam habeas requiem.* In English: "May the angels lead you into paradise; may the martyrs receive you at your arrival and lead you to the holy city Jerusalem. May choirs of angels receive you and with Lazarus, once (a) poor (man), may you have eternal rest." The reference to Lazarus takes us to the Gospel of Luke 16:19–31, the parable of the rich man and Lazarus. We read in verse 22, "When the poor man [Lazarus] died [he] was carried away by angels to be with Abraham." The choirs of angels are petitioned to lead the deceased, like Lazarus, into communion with God, "into Paradise." This is an immensely moving and comforting anthem, especially when it is sung. It is to this anthem, echoed in Shakespeare's *Hamlet*, that the fictional Professor Ashford alludes, as mentioned in the second chapter. The custodial care of the angels takes us all the way.

JOHN HENRY NEWMAN AND
THE DREAM OF GERONTIUS

Newman's epic poem, although not liturgy, is a magnificent description of both the fears and the convictions of an old Christian man, Gerontius, as he is dying and preparing to leave this world.[12] Although not with respect to Newman's poem, biblical scholar John McKenzie writes, "In the Christian liturgy Michael is the protector of the church and the angel who escorts the souls of the departed into heaven, a *psychopompus*."[13] In the *Dream* we find Newman's guardian angel in the role of psychopompus, leading Gerontius home to God. When Gerontius is on the point of death, he meets an angel who sings,

My Father gave in charge to me
This child of earth
E'en from its birth,
To serve and save,
Alleluia,
And saved is he.

The angel who has cared for Gerontius throughout life as his guardian angel now has the task of greeting him and taking him "home" from earth to heaven. "The angel who accompanies invisibly in life appears at the moment of death. In this way the figure of the guardian angel links the believer's trust in God's providence throughout life with his or her hope in God's mercy beyond death."[14]

CONCLUSION

Now perhaps we may see more clearly what Cornelius Ernst was talking about when at the beginning of this chapter he is cited as seeing the angels in the liturgy. The angels are unseen, but not unreal. They are expressions of God's loving concern for us, all the way to the end of our earthly lives.

By way of conclusion perhaps we may say a little more. In terms of the liturgy, the angels, and the mention of angels, "re-direct our worship in a transcendent mode: Interests that run from the therapeutic to the political have so intruded themselves into our Sunday services that the theocentrism of Isaiah's temple has disappeared."[15] These are the sentiments of Reformed theologian Gabriel Fackre speaking of some of the pitfalls of contemporary liturgy. Liturgy is about God, and about God "doing" us, about God inviting us into communion with himself and about our praise of this excessively generous God. It is too easy, maintains Fackre, to let our liturgical assemblies slide into an anthropocentric channel, what he calls "the therapeutic and the political." The therapeutic and the political arguably are important dimensions of and consequences of liturgy, but the primary focus must be God, "theocentrism." That essentially is why the angels are important liturgically. "Singing the Sanctus will not one day give way to something else....Our present worship can be seen as a kind of apprenticeship for what is to come. The worship of God is learned in the doing, by using the angelic language, letting Christ take our thoughts captive and allowing our affections to be tutored by the gentle breath of the Holy Spirit."[16]

Angels in Modern Theology

Karl Rahner, John Macquarrie, and Bernard Cooke

The great temptation of angelology and of every
theology of mediation is to imagine that the
transcendence of God introduces a gap between God
and creatures that must be bridged by a "go-between,"
whether this be Christ, the angels, a hierarchy, or a
sacramental system. This Neoplatonic supposition
overlooks the fact that God's transcendence is
precisely what makes for God's immanence, both as
Creator and in the self-communication that is grace.

Bob Hurd[1]

INTRODUCTION

The seventeenth and eighteenth centuries witnessed the phenomenon that has come to be known as the Enlightenment.
It is a complex phenomenon that requires comment from a

variety of points of view and eludes simplistic descriptions. Having said that, however, a few succinct sentences from theologian Nicholas Lash give us a fine glimpse into what it was all about.

> Truth takes time. For a brief period in the history of Western culture (roughly, the seventeenth and eighteenth centuries) people tended to forget this. Finding all communication unreliable, all authorities untrustworthy, all received wisdom out-of-date, the surest route to truth was to work things out for oneself. The goal of intellectual endeavor was a comprehensive grasp of everything from nowhere in particular. Even today, there are still echoes of this disincarnate myth of "complete explanation," this dream of our becoming, intellectually, "masters of the universe."[2]

Our time and culture are heirs of this Enlightenment. We cannot avoid it. That means, in practice, that we look for a comprehensive conceptual grasp of reality, rather than ongoing and open-ended understanding. If theology is with St. Anselm "faith seeking understanding," then it is understanding we must go after and not rationalistic explanation. This is not easy to do, and often theologians will tend to fall down on one side or the other, "explanation" or "understanding" in relation to Christian faith. As noted in the first chapter, the hope of this book is to follow the line of understanding.

> We must be reserved with speculations about the number, the species, the distinctions and orders ("choirs") of angels. On the other hand, we should

also see that reality is deeper and more comprehensive than a narrowly understood reason suspects. Reality has a level below and a level above without which totality, fullness, and perfection would be lacking in creation. Without angels it would then be materialistically constricted and would not have that mysterious (numinous) depth and height that many poets and thinkers have described. The figurative language of myth is a means of expressing an essential dimension of reality—a dimension hardly graspable in purely conceptual terms.[3]

This passage comes from a 1987 Catholic catechism put out by the German Bishops' Conference, authored largely by theologian Cardinal Walter Kasper.[4] Let us note the various important points made here. First of all, that we should not say more than we are in fact able to say about angels, so that a certain reservation in speech is required. Second, reality is far more mysterious than skeptical and excessively rationalistic minds consider. It is so very easy to think that we have a comprehensive grasp of reality and to refuse the due humble acknowledgment that there is more to reality than our thinking and individual perspectives allow. Third, angels highlight the elusive and mysterious depths of reality that so often escape our pusillanimous minds. Fourth, and finally, language about angels is of necessity poetic and mythical, that is to say, expressed in carefully crafted suggestive language rather than in hard quantitative analytical terms. This carefully crafted paragraph of Walter Kasper's serves as a fine introduction to our consideration of three theologians writing about angels: Karl Rahner, SJ (1904–1984), John Macquarrie (1919–2007), and Bernard Cooke (1922–2013). Each of them has written about angels illustrating, each in his own way, the points made in the introductory citation from Walter Kasper.

KARL RAHNER, SJ (1904–1984)

Karl Rahner's theological prose is often very dense and to some extent opaque. This seems to me to be the result of both his unrestricted intellectual and philosophical curiosity and also his enormous respect for the entire history of the Christian tradition. This can make his writing quite challenging for the average theological reader. However, it is important to say that struggling with Rahner's categories as we reach toward satisfying theological responses is always rewarding. Thus, he admits quite readily that his exploration of angels is marked by a "somewhat high-sounding nomenclature."[5]

Rahner's awareness of the Christian tradition leads him to recognize very clearly the dangers of excessive speculation when it comes to angels and demons. "The speculative angelology of Christian theology has, of course, been enriched (especially in the Middle Ages) by many philosophical ideas and theories which are certainly not binding in faith. The doctrine of demons has certainly led in practice in Christian life to terrible abnormalities, including the horrors of the witch trials."[6] This is a healthy beginning and indeed a warning as he sets out systematically to explore the meaning of angels. Having acknowledged the dangers of too much speculation on angels/demons, Rahner proceeds to outline what he sees as three basic positions in contemporary theology.

"The first view is that the doctrine of created (definitively) good and (definitively) evil personal spiritual beings, alongside and above man (including their influence on the calamitous history of the human world), is a strictly binding truth of faith which must be unconditionally upheld even today."[7] Very interesting wording here—"must be unconditionally upheld even today." Right away, then, this first view insists that Catholics may not simplistically dismiss the reality of angels. "The defenders of a second position today deny forthrightly and unequivocally the existence of the devil and the demons. They insist that the doctrine of the devil has entered into Scripture from outside, that an exact historical-critical exegesis shows that Scripture does not teach but only assumes the existence of the devil and demons (and angels)...."[8] Those who espouse this position, he maintains, need to be reminded "that it is very difficult epistemologically to prove the nonexistence of an entity by showing the inconclusiveness of the arguments hitherto adduced to establish its existence," and also that in respect of the demonic "they need to be warned against an innate temptation to trivialize the evil in the world," both points well taken.[9] The third position admits that "it is not unequivocally certain that the traditional teaching of Scripture and the church asserts absolutely and not merely hypothetically the existence of nonhuman, created, good and evil personal beings," and represents a kind of neutrality between the other two positions entrusting "the problem to the future history of faith and theology."[10] Having outlined these three fundamental positions on the reality of the angels, Rahner wants to move ahead by coming at the issue from a quite different angle.

Rahner's different angle begins by reminding us of the almost infinite complexity of cosmology today, a complexity that should provide a certain caution in our thinking.

In the light of such a basic conception of the world (in which the human being is no longer seen without more ado as the center of a world constructed statically around him, as the one who is absolutely and in every respect underivable, but in which he represents a peak and an effect of a world evolution), the question can no longer be avoided as to whether that subjectivity rooted in materiality which we know as the human person is the only one toward which this world evolution of the material cosmos has developed in continually new self-transcendence. This question must be raised in view of the vast immensity of the material cosmos as a world coming to be. If we imagine the cosmos as a world coming to be, and is oriented in its becoming to subjectivity, then it is really not to be taken for granted that this aim has been successful only at the tiny point we know as our earth.[11]

I find this paragraph quite amazing. In it Rahner recognizes the almost overwhelming nature of an evolutionary worldview, a worldview that is continually open to ever new discoveries. To take but one example, contemporary astronomical research would endorse the basic parameters of Rahner's point of view, and, of course behind what he is saying lies the worldview of Pierre Teilhard de Chardin, SJ. The growing immensity of the cosmos reflects the magnanimous creativity that is God.

This leads Rahner to the question of the angels, at least as a possibility. "Traditional theology especially, with its conviction of the existence of angels (of angels who have a common salvation history together with human beings), cannot start out from the axiom that in regard to God there can really only be human subjectivities."[12] The axiom that there can only be human subjectivities is cosmologically too parsimonious, too small-minded, in comparison with God's magnanimous creativity. Perhaps we might put it like this—to think only of human beings in this glorious and immense cosmos borders on narcissism. Rahner is aware, of course, that this way of thinking raises at least implicitly the issue of beings on other planets, although at the time of writing, 1983, he acknowledges that this question "is not only unanswerable, but refers to living beings which at least up to now have not been incorporated in our own existential and theological sphere of life...."[13] And so he concludes in this context that "If we speak of 'angels,' it is assumed from the outset that (1) they have an essential connection with the world and (2) they have for us an existential relevance that we denied to possible 'human beings on other planets,' since the existential sphere of life of the latter (at least up to now) does not overlap with ours."[14]

Having opened up the horizons of cosmology to, at least, the possibility of angelic beings, Rahner proceeds to consider their existence in a more anthropological direction. If human beings within the evolutionary worldview represent the high point of the evolutionary drive toward greater subjectivity, there is nothing a priori to deny that that evolutionary dynamic in its upward reach toward greater subjectivity may be found in the angels. "In principle, the possibility cannot be a priori exclude that the history of nature in regard to matter may develop toward such more widely ranging regional and interiorizing principles more rapidly than it did toward the emergence of the human being."[15] Although his analysis is admittedly very speculative here, it must, I believe, be recognized in principle that the mysterious complexity of the cosmos aligned with the mysterious and complex subjectivity and interiority of human beings is open to the possibility of higher intelligences, in other words, the angels. Not everyone will warm necessarily to

Rahner's understanding, but there is a certain definite logic to his way of thinking, a logic that finds its base and foundation cosmologically and anthropologically.

The takeaway from this brief analysis of Rahner's theology of angels in my judgment may be said to be threefold: first, he affirms at least implicitly the importance of historical-critical exegesis with regard to angels and their development within the Judeo-Christian tradition; second, he insists that the reality of angels may not simply be dismissed as a relic of the faith of earlier times; third, within an expanding and evolutionary worldview, combining both cosmology and anthropology, the existence of angels must be admitted as at least possible.

JOHN MACQUARRIE (1919–2007)

John Macquarrie was one of the most significant and influential Anglican theologians of the twentieth century.[16] In his *Principles of Christian Theology* he has a section devoted to "The Holy Angels," and this will be the focus of our attention.[17]

"We have seen that creation can be considered as a hierarchy of beings. All of them participate in Being and tend to move toward 'likeness' to God, but they manifest Being in many different ways and over many different ranges."[18] Right away we get a sense of the magnificent sweep of creation in these opening sentences. Macquarrie then goes on to point out that while humankind "stand(s) at the apex of that hierarchy that can be observed on our planet" there is no reason why we should suppose that this great hierarchy of beings "must terminate with man."[19] He continues: "More than ever nowadays, as we learn more and more of the inconceivable vastness of space and time and of the infinite proliferation of worlds, it becomes a probability of the highest order that there are or have been or will be beings that surpass man in the hierarchy of beings."[20] That, of course, takes us to the holy angels, but Macquarrie makes two important points. First, he cautions against idle speculation into the nature and experience of such higher beings, and second, he acknowledges that "as they have usually been represented, they belong to the mythology and poetry of religion rather than to theology."[21] By using such terms as *mythology* and *poetry* he is not making a contrast with *reality*. Rather, these terms are to be understood as ways, necessarily limited ways, of trying to penetrate something of the mystery of being.

When it comes to angels in the Scriptures, Macquarrie thinks, rightly in my opinion, that it is often difficult distinguish in the Old Testament between references to the "angel of the Lord" and God himself manifesting himself and communicating to human beings. This is probably the case, for example, in Exodus 3:2–4 in the story of the theophany to Moses in the burning bush. With regard to the New Testament, Macquarrie again comes to rather balanced conclusions. He writes, "It is interesting to compare the nativity stories in St. Matthew and St. Luke. In the latter, the angels seem to be represented as actual personal beings who come and go as bearers of divine messages; but in the former they appear in dreams, and it is the dream that is the vehicle for the communication." His concluding reflection on these New Testament passages concerning angels is this: "Whatever problems there may be about the usage in particular passages or authors, there is no doubt that the biblical writers did believe in a higher order of beings whom they called 'angels' and who are well described as 'ministering spirits sent forth to serve' (Hebrews 1:14)."[22]

While he thinks that St. Thomas Aquinas's treatment of angels may be remote and unreal for modern Christians, nevertheless he commends the Angelic Doctor for his commitment to theological analysis in this aspect of creation. Macquarrie's own analysis, and in this he is close to St. Thomas's intention, is that the doctrine of the angels "opens our eyes to this vast, unimaginable cooperative striving and service, as all things seek to be like God and to attain fullness of being in him.... The doctrine of the angels directs our minds to the vastness and richness of the creation, and every advance of science opens up still more distant horizons....The panorama of creation must be far more breathtaking than we can guess in our corner of the cosmos...."[23]

BERNARD COOKE (1922–2013)

Bernard Cooke was a Catholic systematic theologian with a very developed and particular interest in sacramental theology. He had the great gift of being able to communicate complicated theological issues in an accessible and yet enthusiastic way. Read superficially, his book *Why Angels?* may appear to be iconoclastic with regard to the angelic world, but that would not be a fair reading. Cooke writes, "At the very beginning, however, I would like to stress that my purpose has not been to make a firm claim about the non-existence of angels; it is just that I see no need for them and fear that concentrating on them may prevent us from appreciating the saving presence of the risen Christ."[24] He is certainly far from being dismissive of angels, especially as he recognizes that "there is a long, long history of humans believing in and trusting angels. It would be presumptuous and arrogant to dismiss that history as simply wrong and misguided, to assume that we in the twentieth century have suddenly become enlightened. Many of the greatest minds in Christianity, including Thomas Aquinas and Dante, whom I consider to be of unparalleled genius in Western history, have taken angels for granted."[25]

While Cooke is not dismissive, not only does he not see any particular need for angels, but angels may prevent us from recognizing the presence of the risen Christ in our midst. In some ways, according to Cooke, the Catholic tradition has so emphasized the transcendence and otherness of God that it tended to lose sight of God's immanence, God's gracious presence to and in his creation. Writing somewhat autobiographically but also in a way with which many Catholics could identify, Cooke says,

> Perhaps, because God's presence is so mysterious and unbelievable, it was necessary that a devotion to the guardian angel be the first step in creating a sense of divine presence in our lives. Without this "preliminary" experience of God being with and for us, we might not have been able later to glimpse the wonder of God being immediately involved in our lives. So, even if there never was an angel at my side, devotion to my guardian angel was something real and very important in my Christian faith....And just as angels like Michael filled in for the "absent" Christ, so devotion to my guardian angel supplied for Christ not being with me apart from the precious moments of Eucharist.[26]

Briefly, angels and especially guardian angels functioned as a symbol for the divine presence and for God's care for us. If, however, we work at retrieving a sense of God's immanent presence in our midst, the presence of the risen Christ in our midst, then a concern with angels becomes somewhat superfluous. With a recovered sense of God's presence all around us, our spirituality changes. "Presence meant that God was interested in me. More than that, it meant that God was personally with me in friendship and that from that friendship I drew my deepest identity as a person. It meant that I was surrounded by, enveloped by, this love of me as a distinct individual person. It wasn't even that God lived in me; I lived in God."[27] Taking it further, Cooke comments,

> It wasn't so much that the guardian angel—and angels in general—disappeared. What has disappeared is the gap between heaven and earth, which was the reason why we thought there should be angels. We don't need a bridge to God, God is with us. Very truly, "heaven" is here. We are not yet fully into that new life we refer to with the word "heaven"; we will have to pass through death to be completely part of it, but death will not be a matter of going someplace else. If "heaven" is being with God, we already are with God, unless we refuse to accept the friendship offered us through Christ.[28]

This is a very fine and indeed beautiful passage. One may, however, pose these questions: "How many people actually reach this permeative sense of God's presence in their daily lives? Is it possible that in reaching toward this sense of God's presence, practically speaking we need a kind of daily symbol system to help us?" This is where angels come in, and especially guardian angels. The reality of angels mediates for us God's loving presence. Arguably, the Catholic tradition of reflection on angels had this as its intention, to raise up our minds and hearts to the God who is always there for us. "What sacramentality is all about is that God's presence, which gives ultimate meaning to our experiences and ourselves, occurs in our ordinary daily experience. Obviously, there can be more apparent situations of divine presence in some extraordinary things that happen, in moments of danger or discovery or success; but God's presence is not something that comes and goes except insofar as we are more or less conscious of it."[29] Cooke is, of course quite right here. God's presence does not come and go, but simply abides with us, in and around us. The issue is our awareness of God's presence. The fragility and vulnerability of human life requires regular symbolic mediations of God's presence—arguably, not only the sacraments and especially the Eucharist, but a regular structure of prayer in our lives, and a sense of the angels. Other Catholic theologians share this point of view, for example, Bob Hurd, who writes,

Vatican II's call for the full and active participation of the faithful inaugurated a reassessment of this disenfranchisement of the ordinary believer in all areas of church life. As the priesthood of all believers is reasserted and faith as a whole becomes more Christ-centered, the relevance of mediating higher powers (saints, angels, and even Mary) for spirituality recedes more and more into the background. This need not be interpreted as a lack of faith or inattention to tradition; it should rather be seen as a legitimate corrective to imbalances in past theologies and spiritualities.[30]

Yes, there is a need to correct imbalances, and perhaps a greater emphasis is needed on God's immanence, and Cooke is also right to insist that human beings can become "angels" or "sacraments" to one another.

> Each person in his or her specific life situation is meant, through their diverse ministries to the needs of people, to be a "word" that tells God's compassionate care for people, but more than just a "word" about a compassionate God. They are to be sacrament; in their ministries God's own compassion is present to heal and transform. One could say that humans are meant to be angels to one another; but the reality goes beyond that. It is not just that they are "stand-ins" for God, God's legates in taking care of one another. Instead, their ministry to one another is actually God's ministry as well; their care and concern embody God's. If one uses the term carefully, one can say that their ministry "incarnates" God's saving power, God's own Spirit. That is precisely why Christian ministry is a sacrament.[31]

Yet again, it seems to me that one has to agree with these sentiments, but rather than dispensing with angels, perhaps their existence and function can serve to confirm and reinforce what Cooke is saying here.

CONCLUSION

Dominican theologian Rob van der Hart writes, "It is still possible for someone to say that angels are merely imaginative concrete realizations of this sphere of sacredness and holiness and have no individual reality in the sense of being distinguished from one another."[32] Yes, I think it is possible for a Catholic to endorse this position, but not without a great sense of loss. What is lost in my judgment is a sense of God's magnanimous creativity. "Why does God create angels?" Indeed, one might ask, "Why does God create at all?" Here the traditional answer seems to me still to be very persuasive: "*Bonum est diffusivum sui…*"[33] "Goodness, or one might say the love that God is, is diffusive of itself." Goodness is such that it cannot abide being focused in on itself, being concerned with itself, but wants wildly and widely to share being with others. God is so totally and perfectly good, so totally and perfectly loving, that he cannot keep existence to himself, so to speak. He is by nature abundantly generous, generous to a fault, as it were. "Among other things, the angels are a fundamental and basic expression of God's mysterious and superabundant generosity, spilling over into the creation myriads of creatures of different kinds. We seem to be so locked into ourselves as humans that we cannot conceive of God creating anything above us."[34]

8

What about the Devil?

It might be argued that the existence of evil in our world offers a firmer empirical basis for inferring that devils exist than for inferring that mere angels exist...

Kenelm Foster, OP[1]

I do not believe in the devil in the same way I believe in God. Belief in God means much more than acknowledging his existence; it entails, in the biblical sense love and trust, that is, commitment. But I do believe in the devil in another sense; the devil is real. I am even prepared to concede (grudgingly) that he exists.

Richard Woods, OP[2]

THE DEVIL IN POPULAR SENTIMENT AND CULTURE

It would be extremely difficult, if not outright foolish, to disagree with the sentiment of Kenelm Foster that heads up this chapter. Looking back at the cumulative and massive atrocities of the twentieth century—what one philosopher has aptly termed "the century of man-made mass death"—provides a very powerful *apologia* for the existence of the demonic in our world.[3] The *apologia* has been well expressed by the Scottish Episcopal theologian Geddes MacGregor in these words: "That some evil agency stalks us for prey or, in the picturesque language of the Bible, that 'our enemy the devil prowls around like a roaring lion, looking for someone to eat' (1 Peter 5:8), hardly seems so weird or archaic as it might have seemed to those who lived before Belsen and Buchenwald and other twentieth-century horrors."[4] We can add, of course, to these aforementioned horrors the sectarian murders in Northern Ireland, the genocidal strife in the former Yugoslavia, the killing fields of Cambodia, the genocide in Rwanda, the horrendous event of 9/11, and the ongoing terrorist attacks throughout the world. Human beings are capable of doing anything to each other, and they do.

I am writing these words a couple of weeks before Halloween, that is, before our American version of Halloween, not the vigil of the Feast of All Saints. And that is unfortunate because much that surrounds Halloween trivializes the devil, reducing him to a matter of fun, and verifying what Dominican theologian Richard Woods says: "A major part of the current theology of the devil is taken from novels, at least on a popular basis."[5] Woods is thinking of the novels and movies *The Exorcist* and *Rosemary's Baby*, and other such nonsense. These media can be fun for Halloween's purposes, and yet at the same time at least in the popular mind they reduce in a very harmful way what traditional Christian theology has affirmed about the devil. Perhaps that is why the Lutheran theologian Carl Braaten writes, "The idea that there exists a negative personal agent at the heart of radical evil, effectively active in all dimensions within and upon human experience, is widely considered a relic of antiquated mythology that no one believes anymore—except for those awful fundamentalists," and one might add Hollywood moguls and Halloween tricksters.[6]

THE CATECHISM OF THE CATHOLIC CHURCH

In the first part of the *Catechism of the Catholic Church*, paragraphs 391–95, we find what the church teaches about "the fall of the angels." The first thing that one notices about these paragraphs is their brevity. There is not much detail—unlike the representations at Halloween and in Hollywood—and this seems appropriate because the triune God, including the salvation and ultimate destiny of humankind, is at the center of the Creed, not the devil, not the reality of evil. Many years ago, while leading a parish mission in Las Vegas, I encountered two Jehovah's Witnesses who right away asked me, "Do you believe in the devil?" I answered, "No." What I meant by that "no" is that I believe in God, the life-giving God who is spoken of in the Creed. He is the one in whom we put our trust, to whom we commit ourselves now and for all eternity. In that sense, one does not "believe" in the devil. At the same time and hardly necessary to point out, the reality of evil is all around us.

Returning to the *Catechism*, paragraph 391 affirms that since everything comes from God and is therefore created good, "Scripture and the church's tradition see in (the devil) a fallen angel, called 'Satan' or the 'devil.' The church teaches that Satan was at first a good angel, made by God: 'The devil and the other demons were indeed created naturally good by God, but they became evil by their own doing.'" This is an extremely important statement. It affirms two things: first, that all of God's creation is necessarily and inherently good; second, that the devil and the demons chose to become evil. There is a definite insistence on the importance of freedom. Paragraph 392 goes on to emphasize "the free choice of these created spirits," who chose to reject God. In paragraph 394, quoting from 1 John 3:8, we are told that "the reason the Son of God appeared was to destroy the works of the devil." At this point, the *Catechism* does not go on to affirm as even more important that the reason for the incarnation was fundamentally to embrace humankind within God's own communion, within God's very self. Nonetheless, this is implied and is laid out more fully in the rest of the *Catechism*. At this point, the *Catechism* is content to state that the incarnation of the Son of God has to do with the destruction of evil, of we may say, everything that impedes or destroys our communion with God. Finally, in paragraph 395 we learn that "the power of Satan is, nonetheless, not infinite. He is only a creature....He cannot prevent the building up of God's reign....It is a great mystery that providence should permit diabolical activity, but 'we know that in everything God works for good with those who love him.'" While in a sense the *Catechism* does not give us very much "information" about the devil, so to speak, it provides us with all the basic principles that we need for further reflection on this matter.

If we turn now to the entry on the devil in Karl Rahner's 1965 theological dictionary, naturally enough we find him in agreement with what the *Catechism* has to say. "(Referring to the statement of Lateran IV), it is stated that God created Satan and the other devils good by nature but that they became evil of their own accord....These meager data do not permit us to conceive of Satan (as popular piety often does) as an equal opponent of God, or to depict the character and doings of the devils." The devil in other words is not an equal opponent of God, but is a creature, and a creature who chose against God of his own free will. Rahner goes on to say, "In view of the seriousness of saving history it would be untheological levity to look on Satan and his devils as a sort of 'hobgoblins knocking about the world'; rather it may be assumed that they are the powers *of* the world insofar as *this* world is a denial of God and a temptation to man. This view preserves the personal nature of the devils, which is laid down by Scripture and the magisterium, since every essential disorder in the world is personally realized....It also means that the devils as elements of this world culpably close themselves to God...."[7]

May we take some of Rahner's comments further? He speaks of the devil/demons as "powers *of* this world insofar as *this* world is a denial of God and a temptation to man." Rahner's emphasis, if I understand him rightly, is on the devil/demons as *this-worldly* phenomena. In my judgment, that is a very good emphasis. Immediately, it distracts us from the all too present Hollywood and media representations, or better "misrepresentations" of the devil.

THE DEVIL IN THE SCRIPTURES

Toward the end of chapter 3 some brief comments were made about the devil in Scripture.

In contrast to later Judaism and much of the literature of the ancient Near East, the Bible exercises "extreme restraint, limiting itself to informing us of the existence of this personage and of his wiles, and of the means to fortify ourselves against them."[8]

Although there is nothing wrong with a Christian interpretation of Genesis, it is simply not the case that the serpent in the account of the Fall was originally identified with Satan. Apart from his ability to talk in this narrative, there is nothing in the account to suggest that the snake was anything more than a snake. As the biblical tradition began to develop over generations of reflection, this talking snake becomes identified with the devil, for example, in the Book of Wisdom 2:24 where we read, "Through the devil's envy death entered the world...."

Judaism believed in the fall of the angels, found especially in the apocalyptic literature, and particularly the Books of Enoch. In Jewish thought there were two lines of thinking about the fall of the angels: that the fall of the angels was due to pride; that the fall of the angels was due to sexual transgression. The idea that the angelic fall was due to pride gathered especially around the name of Lucifer, literally in Latin "the light bringer," the idea being that that there was civil war in heaven, some angels rose against God and were cast out, and Lucifer was the leader of the rebellious angels. The key text in this regard is Isaiah 14:12–15:

> How you are fallen from heaven,
> O Day Star, Son of Dawn!
> How you are cut down to the ground,
> you who laid the nations low!
> You said in your heart,
> "I will ascend to heaven;
> I will raise my throne
> above the stars of God;

I will sit on the mount of assembly
  on the heights of Zaphon;
I will ascend to the tops of the clouds,
  I will make myself like the Most High."
But you are brought down to Sheol,
  to the depths of the Pit.

In its original location in the prophet Isaiah this text is part of a taunt-song against the King of Babylon, the great arch-enemy of the Israelites. The prophet Isaiah applies to the King of Babylon a Canaanite myth of a god who aspired to ascend the mountain of the gods and make himself equal to the higher supreme God Elyon. For this presumption this lesser Canaanite god was cast down to the netherworld. This god's name in the Canaanite myth cited by Isaiah is in "Day Star, in Hebrew *Heylel*, literally 'shining one,' from the Hebrew verb *halal*, 'to shine.'"[9] *Heylel* was translated in the Latin Bible as *Lucifer* and in the Septuagint as *Heosphoros*. So, Lucifer came to be a name for the Devil, but the name "Lucifer" does not appear in the Book of Genesis or the Book of Revelation. As the Christian tradition began to develop in its own right, some patristic writers saw in this passage of Isaiah an account of the fall of Satan. This was especially the case with Origen of Alexandria (ca. 184–ca. 253) who has been described as "the most inventive diabologist of the entire Christian tradition" and who "did much to fix traditional views of the devil."[10] For Origen, the devil and his angels will eventually repent and be reconciled to God, a view condemned by the Synod of Constantinople in 543.

The idea that the fall of the angels was the result of sexual transgression derives from a very strange reference in Genesis 6:1–2: "When people began to multiply on the face of the ground, and daughters were born to them, the *sons of*

God (in Hebrew *bene ha-elohim* saw that they were fair; and they took wives for themselves of all that they chose...." Some have thought that the "sons of God" here are angels. but this seems very unlikely. The admittedly obscure reference seems to be to "giants," a common feature in ancient cultures and folklore where mortals were seduced by the immortals. This view passed into later Jewish and Christian traditions so much so that many of the fathers of the church accepted this view of the angels' fall through lust.

In the Book of Revelation, chapters 12 and 20, we find the most detailed account of the devil's persecution of the church in the New Testament. Revelation 12:7–12 reads as follows:

> And war broke out in heaven; Michael and his angels fought against the dragon. The dragon and his angels fought back, but they were defeated, and there was no longer any place for them in heaven. The great dragon was thrown down, that ancient serpent, who is called the Devil and Satan, the deceiver of the whole world—he was thrown down to the earth, and his angels were thrown down with him.
>
> Then I heard a loud voice in heaven, proclaiming,
>
> "Now have come the salvation and the power
> and the kingdom of our God
> and the authority of his Messiah,
> for the accuser of our comrades has been thrown
>   down,
> who accuses them day and night before our God.
> But they have conquered him by the blood of the Lamb
> and by the word of their testimony,

for they did not cling to life even in the face of death.
Rejoice then, you heavens
    and those who dwell in them!
But woe to the earth and the sea,
    for the devil has come down to you
with great wrath,
    because he knows that his time is short!"

In this text, this apocalyptic text, we are told, using pictorial terms, that war breaks out in heaven, and that Michael casts the devil from heaven. The terms are to be taken seriously but not literally. That is how apocalyptic literature works, as we have already noted. Take note, however, especially of verse 11, where it really is the power of Jesus's cross that brings about the victory over the forces of evil. "Michael's victory is simply the heavenly and symbolic counterpart of the earthly reality of the cross....Michael is the staff officer who removes Satan's flag from the heavenly map because the real victory has been won on Calvary."[11]

Let's try to take this a little further. The fall of the angels as considered here has traditionally had to do with the sin of pride, or the sin of sexual lust, and the "war in heaven" has to do with the refusal to adore God and his Christ. Each one of these issues has a hugely destructive quality about it, destructive in the sense that each one of these issues has the power to lead to the utter diminishment of persons. First of all, pride is a refusal of communion. In the Garden of Eden, the mythical but all too real Adam and Eve refused communion with God in refusing to listen to what God had to say. They chose to eat of the forbidden fruit and that choice was a refusal of communion with God. However it did not stop there. The refusal of communion with God led to the refusal of communion with one another—Adam blames Eve, Eve blames the serpent, and then their progeny refused communion in killing one another—Cain and Abel, and so the tradition of refusal of communion among human beings gains momentum through history. The demonic is the preference for egocentric autonomy over communion with others. We could say that the devil is the symbol of that. What about sexual lust? I don't think that anyone will dispute the fact that the gift of sexuality is a wonderful gift of God to his people. It both conjoins two people in the deepest possible intimacy and also provides for the continuation of humankind. In that respect it needs no further comment. At the same time, experience tells us that sexuality can get us into extraordinary difficulties—it can lead to unwanted pregnancies, it can lead to the abuse of women and men, it can lead to hideous degrees of pornographic satisfaction, and so forth. So, unbridled and undirected and uncommitted sexuality, sexual lust, is immensely destructive of the flourishing of human beings. We could say that the devil is a symbol of that also. Wars and rumors of wars are always with us as we act out our narrow-minded tribalism and enmities against one another. History provides the record, not so much of victors and victims as a recognition that all sides in such conflicts are victims. We could say that the war in heaven described in the Book of Revelation is at least as much about our human hostilities and their egregiously destructive consequences as anything else. We could say that the devil is a symbol of war and its consequences. As a summary of what I am trying to say, let me call upon very astute observations of the Dominican theologians Aidan Nichols and Richard Woods. This is what Nichols says: "The devil and his angels are present wherever there is disintegration of God's creative work, wherever what should be orderly, harmonious, a unity, begins to fall into chaos and anarchy....Their thoroughgoing, clear-sighted commitment to evil makes them not only the disintegration of others but, more profoundly, disintegrated beings themselves."[12] And Richard Woods adds, as it were, "The devil is, indeed, the supreme individualist....The devil symbolizes absolute alienation—the conscious, deliberate rejection of fellowship, the preference for self above all else, as if the whole meaning of existence was contained within the confines of one's own ego....The reward of selfishness is—oneself."[13]

CONCLUSION

Have I reduced the devil to the level of symbol? My answer is yes, but "symbol" is not opposed to "real." Personally, I find it enormously difficult to conceive that any angelic being enjoying the loving presence of God in all its fullness could ever find themselves in opposition to this Love-that-will-not-let-us-go. That just does not make sense to me. At the same time, as has already been stated, evil is all too real, but the greatest evils are those that we human beings perpetrate upon one another. I find myself in complete agreement with the theological position of Carl Braaten:

> Why not view the devil then as the focal point and unifying force that exploits human faults and drives them into destructive and death-dealing orgies?...It would be simplistic mythology to think of demons, or the devil himself, as beings flitting about in the air. We should rather think of them as the spiritual essence of systems and structures gone amuck.... No need to personify demons as little beings in the

sky; they are very much down-to-earth, embodied in economic, social, political, military, and ideological structures of destruction. In our society they are powerfully at work in the media, in journalism, in education, in entertainment, in sports, take your pick....The devil is the source of a magnetic pull toward evil deeply embedded in every individual and the societies in which they live.[14]

9

Conclusion

The basic idea that one creature can be a vehicle of God's gracious presence to another lies at the heart of Christianity.

Bob Hurd[1]

People's belief in angels cannot simply be dismissed.

Bernard Cooke[2]

"Supported by the witnesses of Scripture, the liturgy, and the rest of tradition, the church's doctrinal proclamation has officially declared the existence of angels several times (DS 455–457, 800, 3002)."[3] In other words, the Catholic tradition takes angels seriously. From everything that has been said in this little book, we can affirm that the most proper task of the angels is the glorification of God. In the first instance, angels are about God, and about what we can understand of the things of God. Second, we can affirm that angels have been mediators of God's message to humankind—something that is especially present in the holy Scriptures. Angels are "ministering spirits."

The German bishops' catechism goes on to say this:

The pious belief developed that God has assigned
a special guardian angel to each believer, indeed to
each person. This conviction meets with skepticism
today, especially when trivialized as a false, childish
belief. Properly understood, however, it finds sup-
port in Jesus' saying about children: "Their angels
in heaven constantly behold my Father's face" (Matthew 18:10). This belief affirms once again that
the visible world possesses an invisible dimension
of depth, and that every individual, especially the
small child, possesses an infinite value before God.
The angels are helpers and guarantors for us that our
hope and longing do not grope in the dark; rather,
heaven stands open for us.[4]

David Jones ends his helpful book on angels with these
words: "Talk of angels has always flourished more in folk culture than in official categories. They help illuminate the lim-
itedness of those categories and teach as to be suspicious of
easy rationalism, whether of a secular or of a religious kind.
The world is not tidy, and it is neither fruitful nor honest to tidy
it up artificially. angels help show up the mystery of it all."[5] I
could not agree more. Angels remind us that in our world of
very restricted vision, vision dominated by not so much science as scientism—the view that everything is explicable and
intelligible in empirical and quantifiable terms—"there is more
to the created order than what we actually see, feel, hear, and
taste."[6] Are angels (and also the devil) objective realities in
their own right or are they subjective, more symbolic but real?
It hardly needs to be pointed out that there can be no objective

reality without subjective perception. To acknowledge or to emphasize subjectivity/the symbolic has everything to do with "reality." All human beings live within an inherited tradition of beliefs, values, and ideas, all of which are a combination or synthesis of "objectivity or "symbolism." In this regard I really appreciate some words of the Carmelite theologian, Noel Dermot O'Donoghue:

> These beings (the angels) are as real and as available as our doctors, lawyers, bank managers; indeed they are much more available, for we can contact them *merely by opening our minds to them*. They cannot, nor do they wish to, change the great lines of our destiny, however seemingly dark this may be at times, but in all else they are constantly and delicately helpful. They are in my experience particularly helpful in matters that concern human attitudes and emotions and human relationships; again and again they clear the air; again and again in speaking with people in distress I have been marvelously helped by them to ask some key question, or open up some line of thought or emotion.[7]

This little book about angels, while not delving into the philosophical depths of objectivity and subjectivity, comes down on the side of the subjective, the symbolic, but in a very real way.

By way of summary, then, what is my position about angels (and the devil), as I understand these realities in the Christian tradition? Let me attempt to summarize it in a few points.

1. It seems important to acknowledge that angels are there in the two millennia of the Scriptures

from almost the very beginning, even if in the postexilic period they become more prominent as a result of other religious influences in the ancient Near East.

2. A close examination of the scriptural passages that speak about angels lends itself to understanding them in various ways: as manifestations of God's presence, as bringing messages to humans from God, as offering comfort in times of need, as powerful and symbolic ways of expressing God's loving care for humankind, but in all cases the central and key issue is God's loving care for humankind. If this is so, one might raise the question, "Why does God not come to us as he is?" It would be virtually impossible to better the words of Noel O'Donoghue when he says, "The reason is that the Infinite beauty, purity and pathos of God is far, far more than man can take. Were it to bear down suddenly on man's ugliness, selfishness, and hardness, what would be left of the great majority of men?"[8]

3. As the Christian tradition develops after the New Testament, which itself inherits the Jewish matrix of ideas about the angelic world, these various ways of understanding angels and their functions continue, but without any developed systematic analysis. Systematic analysis occurs really for the first time with St. Thomas Aquinas based, of course, on earlier Christian theologians such as Pseudo-Dionysius.

4. Given the great strides made in modern times in cosmology, and in understanding the infinity of

space, as it were, and moving out from a too-narrow anthropocentric perspective—in line with the insights of Karl Rahner and John Macquarrie —the existence of angels becomes at least potentially more credible for modern people, and in my judgment more persuasive, that is, more objectively "real."

5. Beginning from the fundamental axiom that God is Love, that is to say, goodness-diffusing-itself-giving-existence-to-others, to deny the possibility in principle of the existence of angels would seem to be a too parsimonious view of God's creative love. Creation itself is already an act of grace, of God pouring himself out into others so that those others may share in the divine being.[9] God's generous giving of existence to others reaches its climax, of course, in the supreme act of giving that is the incarnation and the whole event of our Lord Jesus Christ. Human beings through the incarnation are supremely privileged to share communion with the triune God, as the Scriptures and the entire Christian tradition affirms. There is absolutely no need, however, to restrict God's creative activity to humankind.

6. Therefore, when we celebrate the angels in the liturgy—in the celebration of the Eucharist and in the liturgical calendar the angelic feasts of September—we are celebrating simultaneously God's loving care for us (throughout the history of salvation as revealed in the Scriptures), God's closeness to us in our own individual lives, and God's infinite creative love.

7. What is intended by Scripture and the Christian tradition in affirmations about the devil/ the demonic is in my judgment best understood as powerful symbolic expressions of the dangers inherent in the gift of freedom. Freedom may be used for good or for ill. The symbolism of the demonic, aligned in the tradition with the desire for absolute autonomy over relationality, with unbridled and undirected and dangerous expressions of sexuality, and with the tribalism that pits humans against one another in hostility, murder, and warfare, is very real indeed.

As noted in the introduction, the thoughts expressed in this book are intended to help adults, most especially Catholic adults, reach toward a more mature understanding of these issues. If these thoughts are found to be helpful, the author will be well pleased. If not, then the ongoing and never-ending quest for the intelligibility of the Christian faith continues, and one could not ask for more.

Notes

PREFACE

1. Cornelius Ernest, OP, "How to See an Angel," in *Explorations in Theology* (London: Darton, Longman and Todd, 1979), 197.

2. Nicholas Lash, *Theology on the Way to Emmaus* (London: SCM Press, 1986), 3–4.

3. John M. Hull, *God-Talk with Young Children: Notes for Parents and Teachers* (London: Bloomsbury/T&T Clark, 1991), 7–20.

CHAPTER 1

1. Rob van der Hart, OP, *The Theology of Angels and Devils* (Notre Dame, IN: Fides, 1972), 16, 18, 73.

2. Aidan Nichols, OP, *Epiphany: A Theological Introduction to Catholicism* (Jackson, MI: Ex Fontibus Company, 2016), 384.

3. Bob Hurd, "Angels," in Michael Downey, ed., *The New Dictionary of Catholic Spirituality* (Collegeville, MN: Liturgical Press, 1993), 38.

4. See "John Henry Newman and the 'Dream of Gerontius,'" in Owen: F. Cummings, *Liturgical Snapshots* (Mahwah, NJ: Paulist Press, 2012).

5. Carol Zaleski, "A Polyphony of Angels: Theories of Celestial Beings," *Antiphon, A Journal for Liturgical Renewal* 5 (2000): 19.

6. Dominic White, "Are Angels Just a Matter of Faith?," *New Blackfriars* 86 (2005): 582–83. Theologian David Albert Jones in his *Angels, A Very Short Introduction* (New York: Oxford University Press, 2011), xv, writes, "In an age that prides itself on scientific rationality, belief in angels seems not quite respectable. Yet these ethereal beings are now the subject of innumerable references, depictions, and allusions in the electronic ether."

7. Nicholas Lash, "Road-Signs, Reflections on the Christian Doctrine of God," in *Faith, Word and Culture*, ed. Liam Bergin (Dublin: Columba, 2004), 105.

CHAPTER 2

1. Karl Rahner, SJ, and Herbert Vorgrimler, *Theological Dictionary* (New York: Herder and Herder, 1965), 20.

2. D. S. Russell, *The Method and Message of Jewish Apocalyptic* (Philadelphia: Westminster, 1964), 235.

3. Cornelius Ernst, OP, "How to See an Angel," in *Explorations in Theology* (London: Darton, Longman and Todd, 1979), 191.

4. The New Testament scholar and a scholar of apocalyptic literature, Christopher Rowland, makes the following comment: "Some have suggested that this development (of angelology) may have been the result of foreign influence, but there can be little doubt that the raw material for such speculation is deeply rooted in the Jewish traditions." See Christopher Rowland, "Angel, Angelology," in *A New Dictionary of Christian*

Theology, ed. Alan Richardson and John Bowden (London: SCM Press, 1983), 19.

5. This list is taken from John L. McKenzie, *The Dictionary of the Bible* (Milwaukee: Bruce, 1965), 30–31.

6. McKenzie, *Dictionary of the Bible*, 30.

7. David Albert Jones, *Angels: A Very Short Introduction* (New York: Oxford University Press, 2011), 3–4.

8. See Bernard Cooke, *Why Angels?* (Mystic, CT: Twenty-third Publications, 1996), 10–11.

9. See, e.g., the outstanding book by John J. Collins, *The Scepter and the Star: Messianism in Light of the Dead Sea Scrolls*, 2nd ed. (Grand Rapids, MI: Eerdmans, 2010).

10. For the various references in Justin's writings, see the very useful essay of the evangelical New Testament scholar Günther Juncker, "Christ as Angel: The Reclamation of a Primitive Title," *Trinity Journal* 15 (1994): 221–50.

11. McKenzie, *Dictionary of the Bible*, 721.

12. The phrase "the prince of the Persians" suggests that a "guardian angel" has been appointed for each nation. See McKenzie, *Dictionary of the Bible*, 573.

13. Cooke, *Why Angels?*, 12–13.

14. Jones, *Angels*, 5.

15. Jones, *Angels*, 7.

16. Jones, *Angels*, 6. Jones continues in this vein on 33: "At the same time as the Jews were asserting their monotheism, they were also becoming more interested in angels."

17. van der Hart, *The Theology of Angels and Devils*, 49.

18. McKenzie, *Dictionary of the Bible*, 87.

19. McKenzie, *Dictionary of the Bible*, 85.

20. For example, see Jeffrey Burton Russell, *The Devil: Perceptions of Evil from Antiquity to Primitive Christianity* (Ithaca: Cornell University Press, 1987) and *The Prince of Darkness:*

Radical Evil and the Power of Good in History (Ithaca: Cornell University Press, 1992).

CHAPTER 3

1. Cornelius Ernst, OP, "How to See an Angel," 188.

2. Russell, *The Method and Message of Jewish Apocalyptic*, 240.

3. Henry Wansbrough, *Introducing the New Testament* (London: Bloomsbury, 2015), 362–63.

4. John J. Collins, *The Apocalyptic Imagination*, 3rd ed. (Grand Rapids, MI: Eerdmans, 2016), 21.

5. D. S. Russell, *The Method and Message of Jewish Apocalyptic* (Philadelphia: Westminster Press, 1964).

6. Russell, *Method and Message of Jewish Apocalyptic*, 237–38.

7. Book of Jubilees 2:2, cited in Russell, *Method and Message of Jewish Apocalyptic*, 241.

CHAPTER 4

1. Jones, *Angels*, 7–8.

2. McKenzie, *Dictionary of the Bible*, 31–32.

3. McKenzie, *Dictionary of the Bible*, 291.

4. McKenzie, *Dictionary of the Bible*, 31.

5. Wilfrid J. Harrington, OP, *Revelation* (Collegeville, MN: Liturgical Press/Michael Glazier, 1993), 28–29.

6. Cooke, *Why Angels?*, 79.

CHAPTER 5

1. Jones, *Angels*, 41.

2. Hurd, "Angels," 39.

3. Rahner and Vorgrimler, *Theological Dictionary*, 21.

4. Jean Daniélou, SJ, *The Angels and Their Mission* (Manchester, NH: Sophia Institute Press, 2009). For a brief introduction of to Daniélou and his theology, see Owen F. Cummings, *Popes, Councils and Theology, from Pope Pius IX to Pope Francis* (Eugene, OR: Pickwick Publications/Wipf and Stock, 2021), 200–202.

5. Daniélou, *Angels and Their Mission*, vii.

6. Daniélou, *Angels and Their Mission*, viii.

7. Daniélou, *Angels and Their Mission*, ix.

8. Daniélou, *Angels and Their Mission*, 107.

9. Daniélou, *Angels and Their Mission*, 108–9.

10. See Owen F. Cummings, "Death and God's Lovely Presence: John Henry Newman and the 'Dream of Gerontius,'" in *Liturgical Snapshots* (Mahwah, NJ: Paulist Press, 2012), 109–21.

11. Cooke, *Why Angels?*, 18–19.

12. Elizabeth Klein, *Augustine's Theology of Angels* (Cambridge: Cambridge University Press, 2018).

13. Klein, *Augustine's Theology of Angels*, 188.

14. Klein, *Augustine's Theology of Angels*, 189.

15. Klein, *Augustine's Theology of Angels*, 189–90.

16. Klein, *Augustine's Theology of Angels*, 194.

17. Klein, *Augustine's Theology of Angels*, 190.

18. St. Augustine, *Sermons*, 57.7. See Roland Teske, ed., *Sermons of St. Augustine* (Hyde Park, NY: New City Press, 2001–2005).

19. Bernard McGinn, *The Foundations of Mysticism: Origins to the Fifth Century* (New York: Crossroad, 1997), 157–58.

20. Mark McIntosh, *Mystical Theology* (Malden, MA: Blackwell, 1998), 45.

21. See Jaroslav Pelikan, *The Growth of Medieval Theology* (Chicago: University of Chicago Press, 1978), 294.

22. Andrew Louth, *Denys the Areopagite* (London: Geoffrey Chapman, 1989), 41.

23. Jones, *Angels*, 83.

24. Jones, *Angels*, 84.

25. *The Celestial Hierarchy* 3:2, cited in *Pseudo-Dionysius: The Complete Works*, trans. Colm Luibheid (Mahwah, NJ: Paulist Press, 1987), 154.

26. This phrase comes from John Macquarrie, *In Search of Deity, An Essay in Dialectical Theism* (New York: Crossroad, 1985), 75.

27. John Macquarrie, *Two Worlds Are Ours: An Introduction to Christian Mysticism* (Minneapolis: Fortress, 2005), 94–95.

28. Pelikan, *Growth of Medieval Theology*, 293.

29. Christopher O'Donnell, *Ecclesia: A Theological Encyclopedia of the Church* (Collegeville, MN: Liturgical Press, 1996), 7. ST 1a, qq.50–62; 107–8.

30. Serge-Thomas Bonino, OP, *Angels and Demons, A Catholic Introduction* (Washington, DC: Catholic University of America Press, 2016). In the summary of St. Thomas's thought that follows, I am greatly indebted to Fr. Bonino's volume.

31. Bonino, *Angels and Demons*, 118.

32. Bonino, *Angels and Demons*, 122.

33. Bonino, *Angels and Demons*, 122.

34. Bonino, *Angels and Demons*, 173–74.

35. Bonino, *Angels and Demons*, 222.

36. *Summa Theologiae* III q. 8, a. 4, as cited in Bonino, *Angels and Demons*, 222.

37. Brenda Bolton, *Innocent III: Studies on Papal Authority and Pastoral Care* (Brookfield, VT: Ashgate Publishing Ltd., 1995), XI.53. See also the very succinct summary of the Council in Eamon Duffy, *Saints and Sinners: A History of the Popes*, 4th ed. (New Haven: Yale University Press, 2014), 148–49.

38. Norman P. Tanner, SJ, ed., *Decrees of the Ecumenical Councils*, vol. 1 (Washington, DC: Georgetown University Press, 1990), 230.

39. van der Hart, *The Theology of Angels and Devils*, 11.

40. Cooke, *Why Angels?*, 77.

41. Hurd, "Angels," 38.

42. Jones, *Angels*, 23.

CHAPTER 6

1. David Fagerberg, *Liturgical Dogmatics* (San Francisco: Ignatius Press, 2021), 65.

2. Ernst, "How to See an Angel," 194.

3. Fagerberg, *Liturgical Dogmatics*, 66.

4. Fagerberg, *Liturgical Dogmatics*, 68.

5. Origen of Alexandria, quoted in Wilken, "With Angels and Archangels," *Pro Ecclesia* 10 (2001): 461.

6. John F. Baldovin, SJ, *Bread of Life, Cup of Salvation* (Lanham, MD: Rowman and Littlefield, 2003), 117.

7. For a fine introduction to the thought of Otto one might consult John Macquarrie, *Twentieth-Century Religious Thought*, rev. ed. (Harrisburg: Trinity Press International, 2002), 213–16.

8. Cited in Bryan D. Spinks, *The Sanctus in the Eucharistic Prayer* (Cambridge: Cambridge University Press, 1991), 206.

9. Spinks, *The Sanctus*, 201.

10. Frances M. Young, "The Great Thanksgiving Prayer," in Stephen Conway, ed., *Living the Eucharist* (London: Darton, Longman and Todd, 2001), 89.

11. Jürgen Moltmann, *God in Creation* (London: SCM Press, 1985), 74.

12. For greater detail on the *Dream of Gerontius*, one might turn to Owen F. Cummings's chapter, "John Henry Newman

and the 'Dream of Gerontius,'" in *Liturgical Snapshots* (Mahwah, NJ: Paulist Press, 2012).

13. McKenzie, *Dictionary of the Bible*, 573.

14. Jones, *Angels*, 71.

15. Gabriel Fackre, "Angels Heard and Demons Seen," *Theology Today* 51 (1994): 352.

16. Robert L. Wilken, "With Angels and Archangels," *Pro Ecclesia* 10 (2001): 465–68.

CHAPTER 7

1. Hurd, "Angels," 39.

2. Lash, "Road-Signs, Reflections on the Christian Doctrine of God," 100.

3. *The Church's Confession of Faith: A Catholic Catechism for Adults* (San Francisco: Ignatius Press, 1987), 92–93.

4. Noted by David Schindler in the introductory but unnumbered pages to the book.

5. Karl Rahner, SJ, "On Angels," in his *Theological Investigations*, vol. 19 (New York: Crossroad, 1983), 240.

6. Rahner, "On Angels," 236.

7. Rahner, "On Angels," 236–37.

8. Rahner, "On Angels," 237.

9. Rahner, "On Angels," 238.

10. Rahner, "On Angels," 238–39.

11. Karl Rahner, SJ, "The World and the Angels I," in *The Content of Faith*, ed. Karl Lehmann and Albert Raffelt (New York: Crossroad, 1994), 184.

12. Rahner, "The World and the Angels I," 185.

13. Rahner, "The World and the Angels I," 185.

14. Rahner, "The World and the Angels I," 185.

15. Rahner, "The World and the Angels I," 188.

16. See Owen F. Cummings, *John Macquarrie, Master of Theology*, Introduction by the Rev. Prof John Macquarrie (Mahwah, NJ: Paulist Press, 2002).

17. John Macquarrie, *Principles of Christian Theology*, rev. ed. (New York: Scribners, 1977), 233–37.

18. Macquarrie, *Principles of Christian Theology*, 233.

19. Macquarrie, *Principles of Christian Theology*, 233–34.

20. Macquarrie, *Principles of Christian Theology*, 234.

21. Macquarrie, *Principles of Christian Theology*, 234.

22. Macquarrie, *Principles of Christian Theology*, 234–35.

23. Macquarrie, *Principles of Christian Theology*, 236–37.

24. Cooke, *Why Angels?*, 73.

25. Cooke, *Why Angels?*, 9.

26. Cooke, *Why Angels?*, 30–31.

27. Cooke, *Why Angels?*, 27.

28. Cooke, *Why Angels?*, 34.

29. Cooke, *Why Angels?*, 55.

30. Hurd, "Angels," 40.

31. Cooke, *Why Angels?*, 59.

32. van der Hart, *The Theology of Angels and Devils*, 26.

33. See, e.g., St. Thomas Aquinas, *Summa Theologiae*, I, 19, 2, *Ad Resp.*

34. Owen F. Cummings, "More Than a Rumor of Angels," *Emmanuel* 107 (2001): 242.

CHAPTER 8

1. Kenelm Foster, OP, ed., *Summa Theologiae*, vol. 9, *Angels (1a50–64)* (Oxford: Blackfriars, 1968), 307. On 306–21, Foster offers an essay, "Satan," commenting on Aquinas's demonology.

2. Richard Woods, OP, *The Devil* (Chicago: Thomas More Press, 1973), 16.

3. The phrase comes from the philosopher Edith Wyschogrod, *Spirit in Ashes: Hegel, Heidegger and Man-Made Mass Death* (New Haven: Yale University Press, 1990).

4. Geddes MacGregor, *Angels: Ministers of Grace* (New York: Paragon House, 1988), 69.

5. Woods, *The Devil*, 23.

6. Carl Braaten, "Powers in Conflict: Christ and the Devil," in *Sin, Death and the Devil*, ed. Carl E. Braaten and Robert W. Jenson (Grand Rapids, MI: Eerdmans, 2000), 94.

7. Rahner and Vorgrimler, *Theological Dictionary*, 127.

8. Stanislas Lyonnet, SJ, "Satan," in *Dictionary of Biblical Theology*, ed. Xavier Leon-Dufour, SJ (New York: Desclée, 1967), 461.

9. F. Brown, S. R. Driver, and C. A. Briggs, eds., *A Hebrew and English Lexicon of the Old Testament*, reissued with additions (Oxford: Clarendon Press, 1951), 237.

10. Jeffrey Burton Russell, *Satan: The Early Christian Tradition* (Ithaca: Cornell University Press, 1981), 123–24.

11. George B. Caird, *The Revelation of St. John the Divine* (London: Adam and Charles Black, 1966), 154.

12. Nichols, *Epiphany*, 388–89.

13. Woods, *The Devil*, 90–91.

14. Braaten, "Powers in the Conflict," 101–3.

CHAPTER 9

1. Hurd, "Angels," 38.

2. Cooke, *Why Angels?*, 48.

3. *The Church's Confession of Faith: A Catholic Catechism for Adults* (San Francisco: Ignatius Press, 1987), 93.

4. *Church's Confession of Faith*, 93–94.

5. Jones, *Angels*, 122.

6. Richard P. McBrien, *Catholicism*, rev. ed. (New York: HarperCollins, 1994), 256.

7. Noel Dermot O'Donoghue, OCD, "The Place of the Angels," in *The Holy Mountain* (Wilmington, DE: Michael Glazier, 1983), 137–38.

8. O'Donoghue, *The Holy Mountain*, 140.

9. McBrien, *Catholicism*, 256–57.

Bibliography

Braaten, Carl. "Powers in Conflict: Christ and the Devil." In *Sin, Death and the Devil*, edited by Carl E. Braaten and Robert W. Jenson. Grand Rapids, MI: Eerdmans, 2000.

Brown, Francis, S. R. Driver, Charles A Briggs, Wilhelm Gesenius, and Edward Robinson, eds. *A Hebrew and English Lexicon of the Old Testament*, reissued with additions. Oxford: Clarendon Press, 1951.

Caird, George B. *The Revelation of St. John the Divine*. London: Adam and Charles Black, 1966.

The Church's Confession of Faith, A Catholic Catechism for Adults. San Francisco: Ignatius Press, 1987.

Collins, John J. *The Scepter and the Star: Messianism in Light of the Dead Sea Scrolls*. 2nd ed. Grand Rapids, MI: Eerdmans, 2010.

Cooke, Bernard. *Why Angels?* Mystic, CT: Twenty-third Publications, 1996.

Cummings, Owen F. "More Than a Rumor of Angels." *Emmanuel* 107 (2001): 235–44.

Daniélou, Jean, SJ. *The Angels and Their Mission: According to the Fathers of the Church*. Westminster, MD: Newman Press, 1957.

Duffy, Eamon. *The Creed in the Catechism* (London: Geoffrey Chapman, 1996), 23–25.

Ernst, Cornelius, OP. "How to See an Angel." In *Multiple Echo*, 187–201. London: Darton, Longman and Todd, 1979.

Fackre, Gabriel. "Angels Heard and Demons Seen." *Theology Today* 51 (1994): 345–58.

Fagerberg, David. *Liturgical Dogmatics*. San Francisco: Ignatius Press, 2021.

Foster, Kenelm, OP, ed. *Summa Theologiae*, vol. 9, *Angels* (1a50–64). Oxford: Blackfriars, 1968, 307. On 306–21, Foster offers an essay, "Satan," commenting on Aquinas's demonology.

Harrington, Wilfrid J., OP. *Revelation*. Collegeville, MN: Liturgical Press/Michael Glazier, 1993.

Hull, John M. *God-Talk with Young Children: Notes for Parents and Teachers*. London: Bloomsbury/T&T Clark, 1991.

Hurd, Bob. "Angels." In *The New Dictionary of Catholic Spirituality*, edited by Michael Downey, 38–41. Collegeville, MN: Liturgical Press, 1993.

Jones, David Albert. *Angels: A Very Short Introduction*. New York and Oxford: Oxford University Press, 2011. First published in hardback as *Angels: A History* (2010).

Juncker, Günther. "Christ as Angel: The Reclamation of a Primitive Title." *Trinity Journal* 15 (1994): 221–50.

Lash, Nicholas. *Theology on the Way to Emmaus*. London: SCM Press, 1974.

Lyonnet, Stanislas, SJ. "Satan." In *Dictionary of Biblical Theology*, edited by Xavier Leon-Dufour, SJ, 461–63. New York: Desclée, 1967.

MacGregor, Geddes. *Angels: Ministers of Grace*. New York: Paragon House, 1988.

Macquarrie, John. *Principles of Christian Theology*, rev. ed. New York: Scribners, 1977.

McBrien, Richard P. *Catholicism*, revised edition. New York: HarperCollins, 1994.

McKenzie, John L. *Dictionary of the Bible.* Milwaukee: Bruce, 1965.

Nichols, Aidan, OP. *Epiphany: A Theological Introduction to Catholicism.* Collegeville, MN: Liturgical Press, 1996.

O'Donnell, Christopher. *Ecclesia: A Theological Encyclopedia of the Church.* Collegeville, MN: Liturgical Press, 1996.

O'Donoghue, Noel Dermot, OCD. "The Place of the Angels." In *The Holy Mountain,* 137–38. Wilmington, DE: Michael Glazier, 1983.

Rahner, Karl, SJ, and Herbert Vorgrimler. *Theological Dictionary.* New York: Herder and Herder, 1965.

Rahner, Karl, SJ. "On Angels." In *Theological Investigations,* vol. 19, 235–74. New York: Crossroad, 1993.

———. "The World and the Angels I–II." In *The Content of Faith,* edited by Karl Lehmann and Albert Raffelt, 182–93. New York: Crossroad, 1994. These two essays by Rahner represent a somewhat more accessible version of his "On Angels" in *Theological Investigations,* vol 19.

Rowland, Christopher. "Angel, Angelology." In *A New Dictionary of Christian Theology,* edited by Alan Richardson and John Bowden, 19–20. London: SCM Press, 1983.

Russell, Jeffrey Burton. *Satan: The Early Christian Tradition.* Ithaca: Cornell University Press, 1981.

Spinks, Bryan D. *The Sanctus in the Eucharistic Prayer.* Cambridge: Cambridge University Press, 1991.

van der Hart, Rob, OP. *The Theology of Angels and Devils.* Notre Dame, IN: Fides, 1972.

White, Dominic, OP. "Are Angels Just a Matter of Faith?" *New Blackfriars* 86 (2005): 568–83.

Wilken, Robert L. "With Angels and Archangels," *Pro Ecclesia* 10 (2001): 460–74. This essay has been substantially and more accessibly reprinted in "With Angels and Archangels," in his *The Spirit of Early Christian Thought.* New Haven: Yale University Press, 2003, 45–49.

Woods, Richard OP. "Angels," 18–19, in J. Komonchak, M. Collins and D. A. Lane, eds. *A New Dictionary of Theology.* Collegeville, MN: Liturgical Press, 1987.

————. *The Devil.* Chicago: Thomas More, 1973.

Wyschogrod, Edith. *Spirit in Ashes: Hegel, Heidegger and Man-Made Mass Death.* New Haven: Yale University Press, 1990.

Zaleski, Carol. "A Polyphony of Angels: Theories of Celestial Beings." *Antiphon, A Journal for Liturgical Renewal* 5 (2000): 19–29.